Few books have the potential to change how Christians view our times, but Doug Cobb has written one. By connecting the completion of the Great Commission to Christ's return through Matthew 24:14, Doug illuminates the prophetic significance of our generation. His careful research reveals that what seemed impossible for 2,000 years—reaching every nation, language, and place with the gospel—is now within reach. In this book, Doug masterfully weaves together biblical theology, missional strategy, and prophetic insight to create a compelling case that we are living in the most significant moment in church history. The result is a book that will ignite your passion for global missions and deepen your expectation for Christ's return.

Kyle Idleman
Senior Pastor, Southeast Christian Church
Author, Every Thought Captive, Not a Fan, and Gods at War

In his new book *The Sprint to the Finish: The Global Push to Finish the Great Commission*, Doug Cobb brings us into not only his personal journey and convictions, but into God's biblical promise that every tongue, tribe, people and nation will be represented at the throne of grace. Doug's dogged commitment to partnering with God and challenging us to do the same is not only bringing people to the kingdom in the present but may very well help us all see the coming of the Lord in our lifetime, in this generation.

Jimmy Seibert
Senior Pastor, Antioch Church
Author, *Passion and Purpose: Believing the Church Can Still Change the World*

The recent surveys of American Christians have exposed a profound situation. In the 1st Century, the early church was mobilized around the Great Commission, entrusted by the Lord Jesus to His followers. Knowledge and engagement was powerful: because they acted in obedience, the church exploded across the known world. Fast forward to the 21st Century church: in America, a shocking minority can even cite the Great Commission, and fewer still are acting on that divine imperative.

Doug Cobb is not among the ignorant minority, nor is he a Christian who knows much yet does little. I've known Doug for decades: I've watched him turn the final instructions from Jesus into a compelling mission to take the Gospel to the ends of the earth. This book has the potential to stimulate the Holy Spirit's motivation, deep in your soul, to join forces with today's Jesus followers who are working to complete the Great Commission!

Bob Shank
Founder
The Master's Program

The Sprint to Finish by my friend and coworker Doug is a must read book by every follower of Jesus. The book masterfully brings together the Old and the New Testaments, important highlights from the 2000 years of church history, and what the Holy Spirit is doing today around the world, and all in relation to God's eternal plan to save people from all the nations of the earth. In addition to his contagious conviction, Doug has a unique and strong voice of calling us to intimately walk with Jesus, understand the times, and be actively involved in accelerating the Great Commission, not tomorrow but now.

Bekele Shanko
President
Global Alliance for Church Multiplication

This isn't just a book—it's a wake-up call. From Genesis to Revelation, from Abraham's promise to the final celebration around the throne, this book traces God's unstoppable mission and dares you to believe the Great Commission can be finished in our lifetime. It's urgent and it's personal. You'll see the finish lines clearly as you read: believers in every nation, the Bible in every language, and Churches in every place the people live—and you'll realize you have a lane to run. Read it, and you won't see missions as someone else's job. You'll feel the weight, the joy, and the fire to run until the task is complete.

Jared Nelms
President & CEO
The Timothy Initiative

Jesus is dead-serious about the Great Commission, and he wants you to know about it and to invest your life in its fulfillment. Through this book my friend Doug Cobb will help you understand what the Great Commission is and find your place in the sprint to its finish.

Dr. Roy L. Peterson
Former President, Wycliffe Bible Translators
Former President, American Bible Society

I am thrilled with Doug Cobb's new book, *The Sprint to the Finish: The Global Push to Finish the Great Commission in this Generation.* Thank you, Doug, for writing such a comprehensive work that made my heart pound and for helping us see the finish line. This is going to happen. Let's Go!

Tom Doyle
Best Selling Author of *Dreams and Visions-Is Jesus Awakening the Muslim World?*
CEO and Co-Founder of Uncharted Ministries

The media is saturating us with bad news, but *The Sprint to the Finish* will encourage you with the good news of what God is doing to ensure that everyone everywhere has an opportunity to know Jesus.

Erik Laursen
CEL, New Covenant Missions

What first struck me about *The Sprint to the Finish* is that Doug Cobb has gone deeper into the topic of the Great Commission than any other author I've read. With clarity and heartfelt conviction, Doug shows us how the mission Jesus gave His followers is not only still active today—it's completion is both urgent and imminent.

As ambassadors of Christ, God's people called to represent His heart to the nations, and understanding the state of the Great Commission today is vital to living out that role. Doug and I share a deep longing to see every people group reached with the gospel, and this book is a powerful resource to awaken, inform, and inspire the Church to run with purpose in these final laps of the race.

Kurt Nelson
CEO, East-West Ministries

It often feels as though the incredible work the Lord is doing globally is the world's best kept secret. Many Christians have no idea that the Lord is on the move in the hardest places on earth! Not only is he at work but every believer has a responsibility to participate. Doug has years of experience and a unique insight into this work! You will be encouraged and challenged to get involved!

Scott Cheatham
President and CEO, e3 Partners

Jesus left us very clear instructions for what we should be doing while we wait for his certain return. Regrettably, somewhere in all the noise of modern-day life, we've lost our way.

Thankfully, our friend Doug Cobb has laid out in these pages a clear reminder of not only what we lost in our understanding of the Great Commission but also how you can participate in completing it.

David Reeves
President and CEO, unfoldingWord

Clear, concise, and compelling—this book gives the biblical foundation, mission history, and the latest global trends in one volume. Every pastor, missionary, and believer with a heart for the nations should read it.

Dan Hitzhusen
Global Catalyst, Biglife

Doug Cobb's "Sprint to the Finish" is a timely book. What makes the book hard to put down is his combination of classic missionary pioneer stories with his account of what is going on right now. Doug is personally immersed in this exciting and creative new world of reaching the final people groups, places and languages so he is uniquely placed to inspire the church once more for this "sprint to the finish."

Paul E. Miller
Author of A Praying Life and A Praying Church

THE SPRINT TO THE FINISH

THE GLOBAL PUSH TO COMPLETE
THE GREAT COMMISSION
IN THIS GENERATION

DOUGLAS COBB

FOREWORD BY TODD PETERSON

 DEEPWATER
BOOKS

Cover design by Micah Kandros
Interior design by PerfecType Typesetting
Edited by Marissa Wold Uhrina
ISBN 979-8-9859255-2-4
Printed in the United States of America

To the amazingly faithful men and women
around the world who are giving their lives
to see the Great Commission completed.

ACKNOWLEDGMENTS

Gena, my beautiful wife: thank you for your love and encouragement. You are a great blessing to me and many others!

John Rinehart, Roy Peterson, Todd Peterson, Doug Lucas, Scott Cheatham, and Doug Michael: thank you for reviewing the manuscript, your helpful suggestions, and your encouragement.

Tom Harper: thanks for your encouragement and assistance.

My brothers and sisters in Word by Word: thank you for allowing me to teach the book to you and for your questions and suggestions. I am very thankful for you.

My partners in the Finishing Fund: thank you for your generosity and your hearts for the world's unengaged peoples.

To my colleagues in the ACHIEVE Alliance—Kurt Nelson, Kristen Schuler, Scott Cheatham, Doug Lucas, Jared Nelms, Erik Laursen, David Johnson, Dave Gibson, and J. J. Alderman: it is a great privilege for me to pursue the vision of a church in every village everywhere with you.

My fellow elders at Southeast Christian: the finest group of men I've ever been associated with.

Miss Merriman and Mrs. Bendt: thanks for doing your best to teach me how to write.

CONTENTS

Foreword xiii

Introduction. 1

Part One: The Great Commission

Chapter 1: What is the Great Commission? 11

Part Two: The Race

Chapter 2: First Steps. 31

Chapter 3: Training 41

Chapter 4: The Start. 57

Chapter 5: The Race. 71

Part Three: The Sprint

Chapter 6: Believers in Every Nation 93

Chapter 7: The Bible in Every Language. 115

Chapter 8: A Body in Every Place. 137

Chapter 9: The Great Coming 165

Chapter 10: Media and Technology 185

CONTENTS

Chapter 11: The Foundation of Prayer 203
Chapter 12: The Reality of Opposition 215
Chapter 13: Finding Your Lane 231

Part Four: The Celebration
Chapter 14: The Celebration 245

Appendix 1: How Many People Groups Remain? 259
Appendix 2: Must the Church Complete
    the Great Commission? 261
Endnotes 267
Great Commission Ministries. 279
About the Author. 285
The Finishing Fund 287
Study Guide. 289

FOREWORD

Scripture tells us that God determines when and where every person will live. In Acts 17 he goes on to tell us that he does this so we will seek him and find him. My experience is that as we make ourselves available, he invites us into a Great Adventure where he uses us to help others find him. Sometimes that will be in our Jerusalem, or in Judea, Samaria, or—get this—even to the ends of the earth.

So if you have ever wondered what God is doing in the world today, you can stop. He's helping people find him, for his glory! He proclaims in his Word that he is moving to ensure the whole earth will be filled with the knowledge of his glory as the waters cover the sea (Hab 2:14). And he's laser-focused on ensuring that people from every tribe, nation, people and language will find their way to the throne and the Lamb (Rev 7:9). We know this will happen because Jesus literally says so, telling his disciples the Gospel will be preached in the whole world as a testimony to all peoples.

No one knows exactly when Christ will return, but we do know that our God is going to ensure that every tribe and nation hears the Gospel in their heart language. In The Sprint to the Finish, you will see how God is using his Church, the Body of Christ, around the world to reach the unreached peoples on earth. There are still many peoples where Jesus' Name has never been known. And there is an urgency because tens of millions of people are dying each year without ever having heard of Jesus–let alone having the opportunity for a personal encounter with the only One Who saves.

Amazingly, God is using us to reach them, through our prayers, giving and going—to be his witnesses to them—whether they are in the most isolated corner of the world or—thanks to globalization, technology and travel—in our workplace or driving our Uber. Our job is to be faithful where we are with what we have been given, like our brothers and sisters in the Church around the world. To do this we need to align ourselves with the holy Spirit every day, because we can't do this alone. We need his wisdom, vision, provision, protection . . . and so much more!

My friend, Doug Cobb, is doing everything he can to be faithful to this calling. Prior to this chapter in his life, he has had all kinds of accomplishments. He's been first very serious about being a husband and father, he's also been successful in the business world. But most importantly he loves the Lord Jesus and has obediently aligned his life with God's commands to love him with all his heart and to love his neighbor as himself. He has chosen to "get in the game" and help others around the world "seek and find" God.

Throughout my career—in the NFL, in business, and then as a donor and board member of various ministries—I have wanted to be associated with people who are "all in"—who are willing to pay a price to accomplish something significant, and who work with others because they know they can't achieve their Kingdom outcomes alone. All-in is the only way to win in the NFL, and it is the spirit that has driven the massive acceleration across the Bible translation movement in the illumi*Nations* Alliance with which we have had the privilege of being deeply connected. It is also the spirit that motivates Doug—I know very few people who have so wholeheartedly devoted themselves to using everything they have for this purpose. Doug knows to whom much is given much is required, and Susan and I count it a privilege to partner in the Gospel with Doug and his wife, Gena.

In this book, Doug implores us through his insights and example to be a part of what God is doing to see the Gospel preached everywhere—to see God's glory cover all the earth—to see the Great Commission fulfilled—to see people from every tribe, nation and language find their way into eternal security and peace! God has chosen for us to be alive today, at this amazing moment in history, so let's get to work, together, making sure we are each doing our part!

Iron sharpens iron, so get ready—God will use Doug and this book to challenge, encourage, inspire and perhaps even convict you!

Grace and peace,

Todd Peterson
Proverbs 22:29

INTRODUCTION

What's the most important thing happening in the world today? Some might say the soaring national debt, the plummeting birthrate, or the advent of artificial intelligence, and certainly all of those are serious issues. But if you asked me, I would point instead to the rapidly approaching completion of Jesus' Great Commission.

Why? First, because finishing the Great Commission will be a major milestone in the history of both the church and the world. Can you think of any other task that has been underway for so long, across so many generations, in so many places, in the face of enormous difficulties and obstacles? When the church has finally done what Jesus commanded his disciples to do, we will celebrate God's victory in a race that began 2,000 years ago.

The completion of the Great Commission will also be a great day for the world. When it is done, there will be, for the first time in history, followers of Jesus everywhere on earth. Think of how Christianity has transformed the West over the centuries, and imagine the changes now taking place in the most remote corners of the planet as Jesus' name is increasingly known and honored. What a wonderful day it will be when his kingdom finally reaches every people and every place!

Far more importantly, though, finishing this task will open the door for the return of Christ. In Matthew 24:3 (NASB), Jesus' disciples asked him a very specific question: "Tell us, when will these things happen, and what will be the sign of Your coming, and of the end of the age?" Jesus gave them a long answer that continues for most of the chapter, citing numerous events that will precede his second coming. But right in the middle of all that, he gave them a simple, direct answer to their question, saying, "And this gospel of the kingdom will be preached in the whole world as a testimony to all nations, and then the end will come" (Matthew 24:14).

This is the clearest and plainest prophecy about Jesus' return. When will he come back? Not until his people have completed the task of taking the gospel to the world. For generations, that was an insurmountable hurdle—there was no chance of finishing the task. But if we're only a few years away from seeing the Great Commission fulfilled, could we also be close to Jesus' return? If our generation is privileged to be the one to complete the work, could we also be the generation blessed to witness his second coming? I think we could.

Sadly, almost no one is aware that we are on the verge of seeing the Great Commission completed. In fact, very few Christians even have a clear idea what the Great Commission is and why it is important.

Research published by George Barna indicates that 51 percent of US-based churchgoers have not even *heard* of the Great Commission and that only 17 percent—that's about one in six—can say with confidence what it is about. The numbers are better for older Christians and for those Barna describes as "Bible-minded," but even then, fewer than 50 percent have a clear understanding of this central teaching.[1]

Obviously, if people don't know what the Great Commission is, they won't have any idea how close we are to seeing it completed or what remains to be accomplished. This is a tragedy for the American church. Most are missing the opportunity to join the sprint to the finish because they are unaware that the race is being run.

What's more, knowing the remarkable progress toward finishing the task is a great antidote for the discouragement, fear, and even anger many American Christians feel about today's world. Whether it's politics, the economy, or the culture, everything seems to be in freefall. But when we get a glimpse of how the Kingdom of God is rapidly spreading into the darkest corners of the world, and see that it won't be long—by God's grace—until it reaches *every* people and *every* place, we experience new hope.

I think this is what Paul had in mind when he wrote in his second letter to the Corinthians, "So we fix our eyes not on what is seen, but on what is unseen, since what is seen is temporary, but what is unseen is eternal" (2 Corinthians 4:18). We tend to focus on the visible things that surround us and ignore the vastly more important events that are taking place far away or in the invisible spiritual realm. Paul urges us to "fix our eyes" on those "unseen" things—the expansion of God's Kingdom, the victory he is achieving, the imminent completion of the Great Commission task, and the subsequent return of Christ—because he knows doing so will fill us with hope, joy, and confidence.

I wrote this book for exactly that reason: to help you catch a glimpse of the astounding things that are taking place today so that you will be inspired, encouraged, and motivated to find your place in the sprint to the finish.

///////////

I learned about the Great Commission from my mentor Paul Eshleman. I met Paul through mutual friends in 1994, when he was leading *The JESUS Film* Project. I liked him immediately—he was warm and intelligent, with a big, confident smile. More than anything, though, Paul was driven by the vision of giving every person on earth at least one chance to see Jesus. I was drawn to that.

In that first meeting, Paul invited me to join him on a vision trip to West Africa. For some reason I said yes, even though I didn't really want to go. Like many American Christians, my prayer in those days would have been, "God, I'll do anything you want me to do—just don't make me go to Africa!" But I went, and that trip changed my life.

Not only did God show me more of his big world and how his gospel was spreading across it, but he also connected me with friends and ministry opportunities in West Africa that continue to this day. Most of all, though, over those ten days Paul and I built a friendship. And when he later left *The JESUS Film* to head up Finishing the Task (FTT), he invited me to play a role.

FTT was formed by a group of key ministry leaders to mobilize the worldwide church to complete the Great Commission. Through FTT I learned that there is a real chance—by God's grace—that ours could be the generation to finish that task.

God's Spirit is at work in a powerful way around the world today, bringing in a great harvest of new believers from places where Jesus' name has never been heard. Hundreds of people groups—the Bible calls them "nations"—are hearing the gospel for the first time every year. The Bible is being translated rapidly into every language. The gospel is spreading into the edges and corners, and churches are being planted in the most remote places. The global church is sprinting toward the Great Commission finish lines.

My involvement with FTT led my wife, Gena, and me to begin funding indigenous missionaries to go to people groups in India, Nepal, and Nigeria who had never heard the gospel. We were privileged to hear incredible stories of the first known believers in history from among these groups. Those experiences led me to launch the Finishing Fund, a partnership of generous Christians who are giving together to help finish this task. As of July 2025, the partners of the Fund have helped send the gospel to nearly 800 people groups who had never heard it before. By God's grace, our mission is to see Jesus' command to "make disciples of every nation" completed within the next year or two.

Through my work with the Finishing Fund, I've been privileged to meet many faithful men and women who have devoted their lives to seeing the Great Commission fulfilled. Through them I've learned about the efforts to translate the Bible into all the world's languages and to plant churches and make disciples everywhere in the world through movements of the gospel.

They are pursuing what Rick Warren has dubbed the "Three Bs" of the Great Commission—Believers in every people group, the Bible in every language, and Bodies of Christ (churches) in every place—which I believe describe the three finish lines of the Great Commission race. We'll talk about those finish lines in chapters 6, 7, and 8.

///////////

I've divided the book into four sections. Chapter 1, "The Great Commission," stands alone. It lays the foundation by examining the biblical basis for the Great Commission task and explaining God's purpose in his "every nation, every language, every place" mandate.

Section 2, "The Race," includes chapters 2 through 5 and presents a history of the Great Commission, beginning in the Old Testament, the Gospels, the book of Acts, and finally the 1,900 years from the end of the first century until today.

Chapters 6 through 13—"The Sprint"—describe the current state of the Great Commission, beginning with the "every nation" (chapter 6), "every language" (chapter 7), and "every place" (chapter 8) directives. These chapters are the heart of the book.

Chapter 9, "The Great Coming," describes the ways God is bringing the unreached world to us in the West, even as we are working to go to them. Chapter 10 covers the impact of media and technology. Chapter 11 explores the importance of prayer as the foundation of everything else. Chapter 12 considers the sad reality of opposition and persecution.

The section wraps up with chapter 13, "Finding Your Lane," which presents a personal challenge to join the race through prayer, giving, or going.

The final section, "The Celebration," has just one chapter, which describes the marvelous things that await us when the Great Commission task is finally done—the return of Christ, the millennial kingdom, and eternity—things so wonderful that the Bible says no mind can imagine how great they will be (1 Corinthians 2:9).

At the end of the book, you'll find a list of the various ministries mentioned in each chapter. I've included these so that you can easily learn more about these strategic leaders in the race and—I hope—become a prayer or financial supporter of one or more of them.

Throughout the book you'll also find the stories of individuals who have met Christ through the Great Commission effort. In a real sense the story of the Great Commission is the conflation of all the stories of all the people who are coming to Christ through the effort. I hope you'll be inspired as you read about a few of your new brothers and sisters from the world's most remote places and that you'll be motivated to join the effort to reach even more.

At the end you'll also find a link to the Personal Study Guide and Leader's Study Guide that will help you explore and apply the scriptures and ideas presented in *The Sprint to the Finish*.

So let's dive in. First up, just what is this Great Commission?

PART ONE

The Great Commission

CHAPTER 1

What Is the Great Commission?

So what is the Great Commission? Simply put, it is Jesus' command to take the gospel to the entire world. More than that, though, it is the finish line toward which the church has been striving for 2,000 years. And it is the goal to which all history has been pointing, as God has worked through the centuries to gather "for himself a people that are his very own" (Titus 2:14) from every nation and every language and every place.

THE BIBLICAL FOUNDATION

The Great Commission appears in all four Gospels and in Acts. Probably the best-known and most-quoted expression is found in Matthew 28:18–20:

> Then Jesus came to them and said, "All authority in heaven and on earth has been given to me. Therefore go and make disciples of all nations, baptizing them in the name of the Father and of the Son and of the Holy Spirit, and teaching

them to obey everything I have commanded you. And surely I am with you always, to the very end of the age."

These are the last words of Jesus recorded by Matthew. In them Jesus proclaimed his supreme authority and promises to be with his people "until the end of the age." In other words, he asserted that he has been given the power to see his mission completed and promises to be with us, empowering and enabling us, until it is done.

Don't miss that Jesus was speaking to his disciples and giving them responsibility for accomplishing this task. They were to go, make disciples, and teach. And as we'll see in chapter 4, that's exactly what they did. But the task was not just for those first believers. From them, it has been passed along to all believers of every generation, right down to us today.

> Jesus commanded His people to "go," meaning that they are to leave the places where the gospel has been preached and go to the places where it has not.

What specifically did Jesus say his people should do? First, he commanded us to "go," meaning that we are to leave the places where the gospel has been preached and go to the places where it has not.

I've often said that the most important word in this verse is *go*. When we go, Jesus goes with us, and amazing things can and do occur. But until we go, usually little happens.

He also gave a specific target for our going: to "all nations." And he told us what to do when we arrive: make "disciples." This goes beyond merely preaching and making converts to raising up faithful followers who learn to "obey everything I have commanded you."

The phrase "all nations" can be confusing, because when we hear the word *nation* we think of a country—England or India or Germany. But that's not what Jesus meant. The Greek word translated "nation" is *ethnos* (plural *ethne*), from which we get English words like *ethnic* and *ethnicity*. It describes not a country but a group of people who share a common culture, geography, language, ancestry, and so on—an ethnic or ethnolinguistic people group.

There are more than 12,000 of these *ethne* around the world. Some are enormous—the largest, the Han Chinese, has a population exceeding one billion. Others, like the Kryz people of Azerbaijan, are tiny, with a population of only 5,000 or so.

The "every nation" aspect of the Great Commission implies that it is fundamentally a cross-cultural task. It's much more than just evangelism of those who don't know Jesus—although that is very important. It's about deliberately taking the gospel to people groups who have never heard it. The church began with Jewish-background believers and spread from them to the various people groups of the Roman world, then to the rest of Europe, to the Americas, and finally to Africa and Asia. At each step along the way, the good news was communicated from one people group that had received it across a cultural boundary to another group that had not.

Once the gospel enters a particular people group, it can spread more easily, but the first step always involves overcoming cultural barriers. Sometimes those barriers are very high, as when the first Europeans went to Africa and Asia with the gospel. Today, they are often lower, as indigenous missionaries from one people group go to nearby groups with similar cultures: Indian believers to Indian people groups, Laotian to Laotian, and so on.

Twelve thousand or more people groups dispersed across the globe, and Jesus has commanded his church to go to every one of them, preach the good news, and make disciples. That's a Herculean task that, humanly speaking, would be impossible. But Jesus gave us his authority and has promised to go with us, making even this enormous undertaking possible.

And it is happening. The Wulu[1] are a small people group who live on an island in a Southeast Asian country. For centuries they have practiced syncretic Sunni Islam, combining Islam with witchcraft. But not long ago, Pablo—a Wulu fisherman and sometime witchdoctor—met a Jesus-follower from a nearby people group. The man showed Pablo from the Hadith that Isa Al-Masih (Jesus) will judge the world and shared from the Bible that he is the Savior of the world. Pablo was shocked, and his spiritual eyes were opened. Not many days later, he gave his life to Jesus and became the first known Wulu believer.

The word "nation" describes not a country but an ethnolinguistic people group.

He immediately surrendered his amulets to be burned and began sharing his new faith. Many family members, including his wife and children, have now been baptized. Several of Pablo's friends have also believed, and one woman has been delivered from demon possession. Today more than forty Wulu are followers of Jesus.

Luke 24

Luke's expression of the Great Commission is found in Luke 24:46–49.

> He told them, "This is what is written: The Messiah will suffer and rise from the dead on the third day, *and repentance for the forgiveness of sins will be preached in his name to all nations, beginning at Jerusalem.* You are witnesses of these things. I am going to send you what my Father has promised; but stay in the city [Jerusalem] until you have been clothed with power from on high."

As in Matthew, in Luke these words are found at the very end of Jesus' earthly ministry. Again, the task was assigned to the apostles: "*You* are witnesses of these things." And again, Jesus promised his presence through the Holy Spirit, the gift that "my Father has promised." The task is framed a little differently here, with emphasis on "repentance for the forgiveness of sins," but we see again the importance of going—from Jerusalem to "all nations."

John 20

John's version of the Great Commission is found in John 20:21–23:

> Again Jesus said, "Peace be with you! As the Father has sent me, I am sending you." And with that he breathed on them and said, "Receive the Holy Spirit. If you forgive anyone's sins, their sins are forgiven; if you do not forgive them, they are not forgiven."

John's version is the shortest, but it includes the key elements of Matthew's account. Again, we see the importance of going—but John's version frames our going in light of Jesus' incarnation: "As the Father has sent me, I am *sending you*." We also see the power and presence of Christ through the gift of the Holy Spirit.

Mark 16

Mark's account of the Great Commission is found in Mark 16:15–18 (ESV):

> He said to them, "Go into all the world and proclaim the gospel to the whole creation. Whoever believes and is baptized will be saved, but whoever does not believe will be condemned. And these signs will accompany those who believe: in my name they will cast out demons; they will speak in new tongues; they will pick up serpents with their hands; and if they drink any deadly poison, it will not hurt them; they will lay their hands on the sick, and they will recover."

Notice that Mark expresses the target of the Great Commission differently: Instead of focusing on *ethne*, people groups, Mark's finish line is every place—"all the world" and "the whole creation." It also promises that miracles will accompany those who go. And throughout history, wherever God's people have gone with his gospel, God has used miracles to validate their testimonies.

That is still happening today. One Sunni Muslim people group in East Africa had been extremely resistant to the gospel. The missionaries who had been working among them arranged for a medical team to visit, hoping for a breakthrough. As the doctors treated the sick and injured, the missionaries prayed for the people, one by one, asking for healing and deliverance. God heard those prayers and acted in a miraculous way, restoring the sight of a girl who had been born blind. News of the healing swept through the village, and by week's end more than 100 had confessed Christ.

> *Mark's finish line is every place—"all the world" and "the whole creation."*

Acts 1

The final biblical expression of the Great Commission is found in Acts 1:6–8:

> Then they gathered around him and asked him, "Lord, are you at this time going to restore the kingdom to Israel?"
>
> He said to them: "It is not for you to know the times or dates the Father has set by his own authority. But you will receive power when the Holy Spirit comes on you; and you will be my witnesses in Jerusalem, and in all Judea and Samaria, and to the ends of the earth."

Here again, the work is presented geographically instead of ethnically: every place, beginning with where they were (Jerusalem), then the nearby places (Judea and Samaria), and finally the rest of the world ("the end of the earth"). This is the clearest statement in the Bible of the "every place" Great Commission goal.

Today this "every place" vision is being pursued through church-planting movements, which have the goal of seeing a church in every inhabited place on earth. In India, hundreds of thousands—perhaps millions—of small house churches have been planted in recent years, bringing the presence of Christ to places where his name was unknown. Similar movements of the gospel are underway in Nepal, Indonesia, Iran, and other previously unreached countries.

Every Language

There is one more way the New Testament presents the scope of the Great Commission task: every language. In Revelation 7:9 we read,

> The "every language" command is the mandate for Bible translation—the effort to make God's word available in every language on the planet.

"After this I looked, and there before me was a great multitude that no one could count, from every nation, tribe, people and language, standing before the throne and before the Lamb."

Notice that John didn't just see people from every nation, tribe, and people but also from "every language." John is careful to ensure that we understand God's intention for his kingdom to include people from every language.

There are roughly 7,400 languages in the world today.[2] As with *ethne*, the size of the various language communities varies widely. Mandarin is the primary language for close to one billion people.

A few other languages—Spanish, English, French, Hindi, Arabic, and so on—account for most of the rest of the world's population. But there are many tiny language groups with just a few thousand or even a few hundred speakers as well, such as Kalanko (maybe 1,000 speakers in Brazil) and Onge (fewer than 1,000 speakers in India's Andaman Islands).

This "every language" command is the mandate for Bible translation—the effort to make God's word available in every language on the planet. We'll cover that aspect of the Great Commission in chapter 7.

THREE FINISH LINES

Taken together, these Scriptures describe three distinct finish lines for the Great Commission race: every nation, every language, and every place.

As we've said, these goals overlap. Because the *ethne* are scattered around the world, reaching every nation is almost the same thing as reaching every place. And because there is at least one ethnos for every language, reaching all the ethne will mean reaching every language.

Why was God so careful to describe the work using these three different metrics? I think it's because he wants us to understand the full extent of his urgency to see the gospel reach the entire world. He wants it to penetrate every people group to the level of the families and clans. But if that isn't clear enough, he also wants it proclaimed in every language. And just to be sure we understand, he also wants it to reach every place on the planet where there are people.

Think of the three commands like layers of fabric laid one on another on a map of the world. Each layer covers some of what lies beneath, but together they fully cover the surface, leaving no gaps or holes. That's how the result is depicted in Habakkuk 2:14: "For the earth will be filled with the knowledge of the glory of the LORD *as the waters cover the sea.*"

These passages describe three distinct but closely related finish lines for the Great Commission race: every nation, every language, and every place.

It may surprise you to hear there are finish lines for the Great Commission. But as we saw in the introduction, Matthew 24:14 specifically promises that when the Great Commission is completed—when "this gospel of the kingdom" has been "preached in the whole world"—the end will come. The Great Commission is a race, and like any race it has a finish line.

We can't know exactly where these finish lines lie. Jesus didn't leave us a list of people groups or languages or villages when he ascended—he just told us to go to all of them. But we don't have to worry—we'll know we're finished when Jesus appears.

GOD'S PURPOSES

Why has God mandated that there be disciples in every nation, every language, and every place? I think there are three main reasons: to glorify himself, to bless humanity, and to achieve victory over evil.[3]

Glory for Himself

The night before Jesus was crucified, he prayed, "Father, the hour has come. Glorify your Son, that your Son may glorify you. For you granted him authority over all people that he might give eternal life to all those you have given him" (John 17:1–2).

Jesus asked his Father to glorify him so that he may glorify the Father. And how will he do that? He said, by giving "eternal life to all those you have given him." And by that he meant all the men and women in every people group and every place throughout history who will receive eternal life through Christ.

How will completing the Great Commission glorify God? For one thing, it will demonstrate his absolute sovereignty. By finishing the Great Commission, God will prove that there is nothing and no one who can prevent him from keeping his promises.

Finishing the Great Commission also displays God's faithfulness. God promised Abraham that through him, all nations on the earth would be blessed. As the gospel reaches the whole world, it will demonstrate God's perfect faithfulness to his covenant promises.

God's purposes in the Great Commission are to glorify Himself, to bless humanity, and to achieve victory over evil.

The Great Commission also highlights God's grace and mercy. In 2 Corinthians 4:15, Paul writes, "as God's grace reaches more and more people, there will be great thanksgiving, and God will receive more and more glory" (NLB). The more people experience gospel grace and offer thanksgiving to God, the more his glory will be known throughout the world.

Finally, the Great Commission's completion will usher in God's Kingdom. When the gospel reaches every nation, every language, and every place, Christ will return, and God's Kingdom will be established in all its fullness, bringing perfect peace, justice, and righteousness to the earth. From that moment on, all creation will reflect God's glory as Jesus reigns forever and receives unending worship for his greatness.

Think about the diversity of the worship God will receive. Imagine thousands of people groups, each worshipping in their own unique way. That's the promise of Psalm 86:9 (ESV): "All the nations you have made shall come and worship before you, O Lord, and shall glorify your name." That manifold worship will continue into eternity.

Blessing for Humanity

In Genesis 22:18, God promised to bless all nations through Abraham and his descendants: "through your offspring all nations on earth will be blessed."

What form do these blessings take? The greatest is forgiveness of sins. Ephesians 1:7 says, "In him we have redemption through his blood, the forgiveness of sins, in accordance with the riches of God's grace." When a person comes to Christ, she escapes the *penalty* for past sins, is set free from the *power* of sin, and is given the promise of escape from the *presence* of sin in eternity.

Forgiveness leads to a restored relationship, peace, and intimacy with God. And not just with God, but with others as we forgive just as we have been forgiven.

Closely related, of course, is the promise of eternal life. Through faith in Christ, there is freedom from death—and, consequently, the fear of death—for all who believe, and hope for a glorious eternity with the Father and the Son on a renewed earth.

The gospel also brings personal transformation, leading people to live increasingly righteous, loving, and peaceful lives. As more people within a community embrace the gospel, the values of justice, kindness, and integrity spread, resulting in a healthier, more just society.

Likewise, the gospel promotes human dignity, proclaiming that every person is made in the image of God and has inherent worth. This understanding elevates the marginalized and oppressed.

All this transformation—of attitudes, behaviors, and values—renews cultures. Harmful practices like addiction, injustice, and exploitation are subverted, while those reflecting God's beauty, truth, and love are affirmed.

For example, often the coming of the gospel to a place will result in the improvement of the lives of the women there, as their husbands begin to practice the command to "love your wives as Christ loved the church." I am aware of one church network among former Muslims that has set as a condition of fellowship that men no longer beat their wives—a common Muslim practice.

And those are but a few of the blessings the gospel brings when it arrives in a new people or place for the first time. Ephesians 1:3 tells us that God "has blessed us in the heavenly realms with *every* spiritual blessing in Christ," so the list of blessings literally goes on and on.

Some today are critical of the missionary effort, arguing that it is a cultural imposition of the Christian West over the innocent tribal peoples of the world. And certainly, there have been cases where the Great Commission was executed with cultural insensitivity. But think of what life would be without the blessings we've just considered. How can we in good conscience withhold the hope and purpose with which God has blessed us from the peoples of the world?

Victory over Evil

God's third purpose in the Great Commission is to achieve total victory over evil. As God's kingdom comes to every people, language, and place, God will completely dispossess the enemy from his position of usurped authority.

When Adam and Eve ate the forbidden fruit, they forfeited to Satan the authority over the earth God had intended for them. Since then, Satan has been the "prince of this world" and his kingdom of darkness has ruled the planet. We see evidence of this in worldwide human suffering and depravity.

The Great Commission is about rolling back the kingdom of darkness and replacing it with the kingdom of God.

But the Great Commission is about rolling back the kingdom of darkness and replacing it with the Kingdom of God. When the gospel comes to a new place, it breaks down the spiritual strongholds that enslave individuals to sin, idolatry, and falsehood and exposes the lies and deception Satan uses to control people.

Often the arrival of the gospel is accompanied by a confrontation—a power encounter between the demonic forces that rule that place and the missionaries who have come bearing the good news. But because Jesus has "all authority in heaven and on earth," ultimately the forces of darkness are unable to resist the power of Christ.

Think about Jesus' earthy ministry. What did he do? He drove out demons, healed the sick, gave sight to the blind. Everywhere Jesus went he was confronting and defeating the forces of the enemy, who were powerless against him. It's the same today—when God's people go to an unreached place in the name of Jesus, that same power allows them to have victory over the forces of the enemy that have ruled in that place for millennia.

Ultimately, each step toward the fulfillment of the Great Commission points to the final victory of good over evil—to the moment when Christ returns, the kingdom of darkness is finally destroyed, and the Kingdom of God is established forever.

IT'S UP TO US

Jesus commanded his apostles to "go" to "every nation" and "the ends of the earth", preaching the good news and making disciples. That responsibility was been passed down through history to us, today's church. Jesus promised that he would be with us "until the end of the age," from generation to generation, empowering us to complete the task—but it has always been the responsibility of God's people to do it.

No doubt God could have accomplished this task faster and more efficiently if he had done it himself. But instead, he has entrusted it to us. Sadly, we are not exactly the best workers; we get tired, fearful, discouraged, and confused. We're slow and foolish—and sometimes just plain disobedient. Given all that, why did God decide to do it this way?

For one thing, because the work requires us to be closely connected with and dependent on him. God desires intimacy with us and knows that we need intimacy with him, and there is nothing like the work of the Great Commission to force us into deep dependence on him. We'll talk more about that in chapter 11.

> Jesus promised that he would be with us "until the end of the age," from generation to generation, empowering us to complete the task.

I also think he shares the task with us as an expression of his great love for us. Because he loves us, he wants us to experience the joy of partnering with him to see the task completed.

Years ago, after Hurricane Katrina, our church held a "house build" where hundreds of volunteers—including many families—prefabbed houses to be assembled in New Orleans. I'll never forget seeing small children, hammer in hand, driving nails like this: tap-tap-tap. Those kids' daddies could have driven those nails with two swings. But were they annoyed at their little ones' slow work? No. They were beaming, proud and joyful that their kids were sharing in the task. I think that's a picture of how God see us—slow and weak, like little children. But like a proud Daddy, he is delighted to let us hold the hammer.

IT WILL BE ACCOMPLISHED

Matthew 24:14 links the completion of the Great Commission with the return of Jesus: "This gospel of the kingdom *will be* preached in the whole world as a testimony to all nations, and then the end *will* come."

Notice that Jesus said "will be," not "might be" or "should be" or "could be." This prophetic "will be" should remove any doubt that the task will be completed. It will be done. The king has decreed it. And even though it has taken nearly 2,000 years, today we are on the brink of seeing that promise fulfilled.

PART TWO
The Race

CHAPTER 2

First Steps

When Jesus commanded his disciples to "go and make disciples of all nations," he wasn't dreaming up some new task to keep them occupied while he was away. Instead, he was commanding them to make true what God had already been promising for thousands of years. It has always been God's commitment that the promise of life through his Son would be for every people speaking every language in every place.

ABRAHAM

The first expression of God's plan is found in Genesis 22, where God tested Abraham by commanding him to sacrifice his son Isaac. Abraham obeyed God and would have sacrificed Isaac, had God not intervened at the last second.

Immediately after this amazing display of faith, God reiterated his promises to Abraham of blessing and descendants and then added a new promise: "*through your offspring* all nations on earth will be blessed, because you have obeyed me" (Genesis 22:18).

"Offspring" here is singular, referring to one particular descendant of Abraham, Jesus Christ. Jesus, who is—humanly speaking—Abraham's many-times-great-grandson, is the one through whom God will fulfill his promise to bless the entire world.

Here and elsewhere in the Old Testament, the word translated "nations" (or "Gentiles") is the Hebrew word *goyim*, the plural of *goy*. It is used over 500 times in the Old Testament, usually to refer to the world's non-Jewish people groups. Its meaning is very similar to the Greek word *ethnos*. In fact, when the Hebrew Old Testament was first translated into Greek, *ethnos* was the word the translators most frequently chose to translate *goy*. When Paul quoted Genesis 22:18 in Galatians 3:8—"All nations will be blessed through you"—he quoted from the Greek Old Testament, using the Greek word *ethnos* to translate *goyim*.

> When Jesus commanded his disciples to "go and make disciples of all nations," he was commanding them to make true what God had already been promising for thousands of years.

THE PSALMS AND PROPHETS

God's promise is repeated over and over in the Psalms and the Prophets.

"Be still, and know that I am God; I will be exalted *among the nations*, I will be exalted in the earth" (Psalm 46:10).

"*All nations* will be blessed through him [the Messiah], and they will call him blessed" (Psalm 72:17).

"*All the nations* you have made will come and worship before you, Lord" (Psalm 86:9).

"Praise the LORD, *all you nations*; extol him, *all you peoples*" (Psalm 117:1).

And these are just a few of the dozens of times that the Great Commission promises appear in the Psalms.

This same theme recurs in the Prophets. In Isaiah 49:6, God promised that the coming Messiah will be "a light for *the nations*, that my salvation may reach to the end of the earth" (ESV). In Isaiah 66:18, God says that he will "gather the people of *all nations* and languages, and they will come and see my glory."

In Daniel 7, Daniel had a vision of the glorified Savior:

In my vision at night I looked, and there before me was one like a son of man, coming with the clouds of heaven . . . He was given authority, glory and sovereign power; *all nations and peoples of every language worshiped him.* (vv. 13–14)

The prophet Malachi declared, "'My name will be great among *the nations*, from where the sun rises to where it sets. In *every place* incense and pure offerings will be brought to me, because my name will be great among the nations,' says the LORD Almighty" (Malachi 1:11).

Finally, Habakkuk prophesied that "the earth will be filled with the knowledge of the glory of the LORD as the waters cover the sea" (Habakkuk 2:14).

All three Great Commission finish lines are found in these passages. And did you notice the words *all* and *every* repeated in these verses? Over and over, God declares that his gospel promises apply to all nations, all languages, and all places. When Jesus gave the Great Commission to his people, he was inviting us to join him in making those promises come true.

ISRAEL

When God set apart the nation of Israel, his intention was for them to share his revelation with the world. They were to make his name great among the nations. Sadly, though, the people of Israel neglected this opportunity. Rather than share their special knowledge of God, they kept it to themselves and even came to regard themselves as superior to the world's other peoples, because they knew God and the others did not.

> When God set apart the nation of Israel, his intention was for them to share his revelation with the world.

Despite the reluctance of his people, though, God was slowly beginning to accomplish his Great Commission. Let's consider a few examples.

Rahab

Rahab was a prostitute who lived in the Canaanite city of Jericho. She famously saved the lives of the men Joshua had sent to spy out Jericho by hiding them from Jericho's king. After the danger had passed, she told the spies that "when we heard" of the amazing way

God had delivered his people from Egypt and given them victory over the Amorite kings Sihon and Og, "our hearts melted in fear and everyone's courage failed because of you, for the LORD your God is God in heaven above and on the earth below" (Joshua 2:11).

Rahab heard about the greatness of God and believed "that the Lord has given you this land" (Joshua 2:9). She asked for mercy from the spies in exchange for her service to them: "Now then, please swear to me by the LORD that you will show kindness to my family, because I have shown kindness to you" (Joshua 2:12).

The Canaanite invasion is not a model for missions—we don't force the gospel on unreached peoples but instead go to them in gentleness and love. Nevertheless, for Rahab the coming of the Israelites was the coming of salvation, as she heard about and believed in the one true living God who could part the seas. As a result, when Jericho fell, her life was spared, and she joined God's chosen people. Her act of faith was honored by God in Hebrews 11, and she became an ancestor of Christ, mentioned by name in Matthew chapter 1.

Naaman

Second Kings 5 tells the story of Naaman, an Aramean general who was struck with leprosy—a horrible, incurable disease. At that time the Arameans were a growing threat to the northern kingdom of Israel, and the relationship between the two kingdoms was marked by border skirmishes, raids, and periodic open warfare.

Naaman's wife had an Israelite slave girl—a captive stolen away from her home by Aramean raiders. One day, this girl told Naaman's wife, "If only my master would see the prophet who is in

Samaria! He would cure him of his leprosy" (2 Kings 5:3). Naaman, having no other hope, journeyed to Israel, where he encountered the prophet Elisha and was healed. This led him to declare, "I know that there is no God in all the world except in Israel" (2 Kings 5:15).

Nebuchadnezzar

The Babylonian exile took God's people into the land of the pagan Babylonians. One of the exiles was a young man named Daniel. Through a series of amazing events, he rose to a position of great authority in the Babylonian Empire—a position God used to draw the great king of Babylon, Nebuchadnezzar, to salvation.

Late in Nebuchadnezzar's life—after seven long years of severe discipline—he "raised [his] eyes toward heaven" and "praised the Most High," to "honor and glorify him who lives forever." Nebuchadnezzar declared,

> It is my pleasure to tell you about the miraculous signs and wonders that the Most High God has performed for me. How great are his signs, how mighty his wonders! His kingdom is an eternal kingdom; his dominion endures from generation to generation. (Daniel 4:2–3)

Nebuchadnezzar met "the Most High God" through Daniel, an involuntary missionary whose faithful, blameless life was a witness to the nature and character of the God he served.

The Queen of Sheba

Another Old Testament example of the Great Commission is the visit of the Queen of Sheba to the court of King Solomon.

We're told that when she "heard about the fame of Solomon and his relationship to the LORD, she came to test Solomon with hard questions" (1 Kings 10:1). As she observed the great prosperity of Solomon's kingdom at the peak of its glory, "she was overwhelmed" and declared,

> Praise be to the LORD your God, who has delighted in you and placed you on the throne of Israel. Because of the LORD's eternal love for Israel, he has made you king to maintain justice and righteousness. (1 Kings 10:9)

When the queen saw the amazing blessings God had poured out on Solomon and his people, what began as a diplomatic and intellectual mission became a spiritual awakening. The praise she offered God was not polite flattery; she recognized that the God of Israel is the true source of wisdom, justice, and blessing—the one true God.

And she wasn't the only one: Later in that same chapter we read, "The whole world sought audience with Solomon to hear the wisdom God had put in his heart" (1 Kings 10:24). Likely there were many visitors to Solomon's Israel who came away transformed by the living God.

Jonah

But these stories are the exceptions. The common attitude of the Jews toward the Gentiles is illustrated by the reluctant prophet Jonah. When commanded to go to the Assyrian capital of Nineveh and preach repentance, Jonah refused. Instead, he went to the port city of Joppa and boarded a boat sailing west to Tarshish—the opposite direction from Nineveh. Jonah hated the Assyrians. He did not want them to repent—he wanted God to destroy them. And he did his best to avoid going to them.

The common attitude of the Jews toward the Gentiles is illustrated by the reluctant prophet Jonah.

But God is hard to resist, and ultimately he convinced Jonah to go. When Jonah arrived in Nineveh, he warned the Assyrians of God's coming judgment, and to his disgust they repented and God relented.

In his anger Jonah accused God of being too kind: "I knew that you are a gracious and compassionate God, slow to anger and abounding in love, a God who relents from sending calamity" (Jonah 4:2). Ironically, this is the very thing God wanted the Ninevites—and the whole world—to know about him. But to Jonah, God's kindness to Israel's enemy was inexcusable.

Even when he was fleeing, Jonah could not escape being a witness for God. As the storm raged around Jonah's boat, the sailors demanded that he tell them who he was and why he had brought this trouble on them. Jonah answered with what amounts to a reluctant Old Testament gospel presentation: "I am a Hebrew and I worship the LORD, the God of heaven, who made the sea and the dry land" (Jonah 1:9).

Ultimately, they threw Jonah overboard, and the storm immediately calmed. Their response? "At this the men greatly feared the LORD, and they offered a sacrifice to the LORD and made vows to him" (Jonah 1:16). God used even the disobedience of his servant Jonah to draw these sailors into relationship with him.

CONCLUSION

Through the Old Testament scriptures, God makes clear that his promises of salvation are for the whole world—every nation, every language, and every place. Having equipped his people with those instructions, he desired them to be witnesses of his goodness and glory to a lost world. Israel, for the most part, was unwilling to do so, but God nevertheless worked through their reluctance and disobedience to begin accomplishing the task.

But the big push was yet to come, when God would assign the work to the church, his gospel-redeemed, Spirit-filled people. We'll look at the start of that in the next chapter.

CHAPTER 3

Training

Before Jesus commanded his disciples to take the good news to every people, language, and place, he prepared them for the task, modeling the work by engaging with people from different cultures, teaching about the every-nation nature of his kingdom, and training them on how to go. In this chapter we will consider the ways Jesus equipped his followers for the Great Commission.

JESUS GOES

Jesus' entire earthly ministry modeled "going." He left the glory of heaven to go into the world. He left his home, his job, and his family to go throughout Galilee for his public ministry. Everywhere Jesus went he brought his kingdom with him and announced its coming through his preaching and with signs and wonders. Although the priority of Jesus' ministry was to reveal his kingdom to Israel, he also prepared his followers for their mission to the nations. So from time to time he arranged encounters with Gentiles to show his disciples that the kingdom is for all peoples.

Tyre and Sidon

Matthew 15:21–28 describes Jesus' visit to the region of Tyre and Sidon—Gentile territory. While there, he had an encounter with a Canaanite woman, who cried out to him, "Lord, Son of David, have mercy on me! My daughter is demon-possessed and suffering terribly" (Matthew 15:22). That title, "Son of David," reveals that this woman understood who Jesus is.

Jesus answered, "I was sent only to the lost sheep of Israel," clarifying that his primary mission was to the Jews, his own *ethnos*. When she persisted, he tested her, saying, "It is not right to take the children's bread and toss it to the dogs" (Matthew 15:26).

Her reply was remarkable: "Yes it is, Lord. Even the dogs eat the crumbs that fall from their master's table" (Matthew 15:27). The story concludes, "Then Jesus said to her, 'Woman, you have great faith! Your request is granted.' And her daughter was healed at that moment."

Before Jesus commanded his disciples to take the good news to every people, language, and place, He began preparing them for the task.

In this encounter Jesus opened the door of his kingdom to this Gentile woman, showing his disciples that it was for Gentiles as well as Jews. He made it clear that God's mercy extends beyond ethnic boundaries to anyone who believes.

The Decapolis

Mark 5:1–20 tells the story of Jesus' visit to the region of the Gerasenes, who lived on the eastern shore of the Sea of Galilee. Again, this was Gentile territory. When they arrived, Jesus and his disciples immediately encountered a demon-possessed man. Jesus cast out the demons that were tormenting him, sending them into a herd of pigs. After being delivered, the man wanted to follow Jesus, but Jesus told him to stay and tell others in his region what had happened to him. The man obeyed and "went away and began to tell in the Decapolis how much Jesus had done for him. And all the people were amazed."

Later, when Jesus returned to this region, the people were receptive and brought to him those who needed healing, suggesting that this man's testimony had prepared the way for Jesus.

This man is an early example of a near-culture missionary—a person culturally similar to those he is reaching, who can relate to his audience in a familiar and comfortable way without cultural or language barriers. Today, much of the final mile of the Great Commission is being run by near-culture missionaries: Chinese believers going to Chinese, Africans to Africans, and so on.

This story also shows how the gospel often enters a new place through a spiritual power encounter. Jesus demonstrated his power and authority over the demonic forces that tormented this man. That terrified the Gerasenes, who sadly asked Jesus to leave them, but it became the foundation of the demoniac's testimony. Even today, healings and demonic deliverances are often instrumental in the gospel penetrating a new place.

The Woman at the Well

Perhaps Jesus' best-known cross-cultural encounter is found in John 4:1–42. Jesus was headed from Judea back to Galilee and "had to go through Samaria." Technically, that isn't true. Jews so despised Samaritans that they would take a longer route, along the Jordan River, when traveling between Galilee and Judea, bypassing Samaria altogether. But Jesus had a divine appointment in Samaria that he intended to keep. This was a mission trip—an example of going to a place that had not yet received the good news.

When Jesus arrived in the town of Sychar, he sat down by Jacob's well while the disciples went for food. As he was resting, a Samaritan woman came out to draw water. When Jesus asked the woman for a drink, she replied, "You are a Jew and I am a Samaritan woman. How can you ask me for a drink?" John adds, parenthetically, "For Jews do not associate with Samaritans." Although they spoke the same language, the cultural barriers between them were sky-high.

The Samaritan woman is an example of a "person of peace."

As their conversation continued, she raised a religious objection: "Our ancestors worshiped on this mountain, but you Jews claim that the place where we must worship is in Jerusalem." Jesus' answer cut through her parry with spiritual truth: "A time is coming and has now come when the true worshipers will worship the Father in the Spirit and in truth, for they are the kind of worshipers the Father seeks."

When she tried one last time to derail the conversation—saying, "'I know that Messiah' (called Christ) 'is coming. When he comes, he will explain everything to us'"—Jesus seized on this fragment of truth saying, "I, the one speaking to you—I am he," revealing himself to her.

When the disciples returned, they were baffled. Here was their master, talking to a Samaritan woman. What was going on? She, on the other hand, knew exactly what was happening. John tells us that she

> went back to the town and said to the people, 'Come, see a man who told me everything I ever did. Could this be the Messiah?' They came out of the town and made their way toward him . . . Many of the Samaritans from that town believed in him because of the woman's testimony, 'He told me everything I ever did.' So when the Samaritans came to him, they urged him to stay with them, and he stayed two days. And because of his words many more became believers.

Think about what the disciples learned during those two days. Despised Samaritans coming to faith in Christ! How was it possible? They must have watched in wonder as Jesus answered the Samaritans' questions and objections and led them into relationship with his Father. No doubt they often remembered those days in the years to come as they carried out their mission to the world.

The Samaritan woman is an example of a "person of peace," someone selected by God to be the open door through which the gospel enters a culture. Later, Jesus would instruct his disciples to seek out just such people when they were on their missionary training trips.

Other Encounters

In addition to these examples, there were other encounters where Jesus demonstrated the value of Gentiles to his disciples. In one of these (Luke 17:11–19), Jesus was traveling along the border of Samaria when he encountered ten men with leprosy. Jesus healed them and ordered them to go show themselves to the priests (a requirement in Jewish law). Only one of the men, a Samaritan, thanked Jesus and praised God for his healing.

Jesus commended the faith of the healed Samaritan, telling him, "Your faith has made you well." Again, Jesus was conveying that salvation is by grace through faith to all who believe—even "a foreigner" like this man.

At another time, Jesus healed the servant of a Roman centurion (Matthew 8:5–13). The centurion approached him, asking for help, and when Jesus offered to come and heal the servant, he replied, "Lord, I do not deserve to have you come under my roof. But just say the word, and my servant will be healed." Jesus was "amazed" at this man's faith, saying, "Truly I tell you, I have not found anyone in Israel with such great faith." He then explained to his disciples,

> "I say to you that many will come from the east and the
> west, and will take their places at the feast with Abraham,
> Isaac and Jacob in the kingdom of heaven. But the subjects
> of the kingdom will be thrown outside, into the darkness,
> where there will be weeping and gnashing of teeth."

In saying this, Jesus prophesied that many from his own nation would reject him, but many from other nations and places would receive him and thereby enter his kingdom. Not only did Jesus affirm the faith of the centurion, but he also held him up as an example of the people to whom the gospel would spread through the Great Commission.

JESUS TEACHES

In all these encounters, Jesus used his interactions with Gentiles to model the every-nation nature of his kingdom. Let's now consider two incidents where Jesus explicitly taught this same truth.

Teaching in Nazareth

After Jesus' forty days in the wilderness, he returned to Galilee and began preaching in the synagogues (Luke 4:14–30). On one Sabbath, he visited the synagogue in Nazareth, where he read from the scroll of Isaiah. After reading the passage, he sat down and declared, "Today this scripture is fulfilled in your hearing," launching his public ministry.

This was not received well by his listeners. "Isn't this Joseph's son?" they asked resentfully. Who did Jesus think he was to apply this Messianic passage to himself? In response, Jesus delivered this short, explosive sermon:

> "Truly I tell you," he continued, "no prophet is accepted in his hometown. I assure you that there were many widows in Israel in Elijah's time, when the sky was shut for three and a half years and there was a severe famine throughout the land. Yet Elijah was not sent to any of them, but to a widow in Zarephath in the region of Sidon. And there were many in Israel with leprosy in the time of Elisha the prophet, yet not one of them was cleansed—only Naaman the Syrian."

This is what Jesus meant: If the Jews would not receive God's grace, he would instead pour it out on the Gentiles. He made his point by recalling two Old Testament stories where God did just that: God's miraculous provision for the widow in Zarephath, a Sidonian; and God's miraculous healing of Naaman, an Aramean.

> If the Jews would not receive God's grace, he would instead pour it out on the Gentiles.

The Jews in the synagogue "were furious when they heard this." Verse 29 adds that they drove him out of town, intending to throw him off a cliff. As Jews, they saw themselves as the exclusive beneficiaries of God's grace and thus superior to the nations. They recoiled at the idea that God could (and would) build a global kingdom embracing multiple *ethne*.

The Parable of the Great Banquet

Much later in his ministry, Jesus was having dinner one Sabbath in the house of a prominent Pharisee (Luke 14:15–24). While there he healed a man with edema, rebuking his host for the Pharisees' rule prohibiting healing on the Sabbath. He also admonished his host and the other guests against self-seeking and pride, teaching them that "all those who exalt themselves will be humbled, and those who humble themselves will be exalted."

When one of the guests—probably to diffuse the tension—blurted out, "Blessed is the one who will eat at the feast in the Kingdom of God," Jesus responded with a parable:

"A certain man was preparing a great banquet and invited many guests. At the time of the banquet, he sent his servant to tell those who had been invited, 'Come, for everything is now ready.' But all the invited guests began to make excuses: 'I have just bought a field, and I must go and see it'; 'I have just bought five yoke of oxen, and I'm on my way to try them out'; 'I just got married, so I can't come.'

"The servant came back and reported this to his master. Then the owner of the house became angry and ordered his servant, 'Go out quickly into the streets and alleys of the town and bring in the poor, the crippled, the blind and the lame.' 'Sir,' the servant said, 'what you ordered has been done, but there is still room.' Then the master told his servant, 'Go out to the roads and country lanes and compel them to come in, so that my house will be full. I tell you, not one of those who were invited will get a taste of my banquet.'"

In this parable, the host of the banquet is God the Father, and the banquet represents his kingdom. The servant is Jesus, who invites the world into the kingdom. The invited guests represent the Jews, God's chosen people. "The poor, the crippled, the blind and the lame" represent the outcasts of the Jewish nation—the kind of people Jesus' host that day would never invite to his house. And the people found along "the roads and country lanes" represent the Gentile world—the nations.

Jesus' warning? The Jewish leaders—those with whom he was dining—would reject the invitation to the Kingdom of God because they were too occupied with worldly things. Some Jews

Jesus was teaching his disciples to seek out those who would receive the invitation, whoever and wherever they were.

would receive it, but only the outcasts and marginalized. And the majority of those in the kingdom would be Gentiles.

Doubtless this story went over like a lead balloon that day. But Jesus was teaching an important lesson to his disciples about his kingdom and their mission: to seek out those who would receive the invitation, whoever and wherever they were.

JESUS TRAINS

Jesus modeled cross-cultural evangelism and taught that Gentiles would be part of his kingdom. He also trained his disciples for the task he would assign them. We see this clearly in a progression of episodes documented in Luke 8, 9, and 10.

Luke 8 begins, "After this, Jesus traveled about from one town and village to another, proclaiming the good news of the Kingdom of God. The Twelve were with him . . ." In other words, Jesus was on a mission trip, and he had taken the disciples along so that they could see what he did and how he did it.

The Twelve

After modeling the work, Jesus sent the Twelve "out to proclaim the Kingdom of God and to heal the sick" (Luke 9:1–6, 10). In Matthew's account, Jesus instructs them to "heal the sick, raise the dead, cleanse the lepers, cast out demons." These are the very things

Jesus himself had been doing, but now he is sending them out, for the first time, on their own. This was not a cross-cultural mission trip, but it was their first experience with "going."

Before he sent them out, Jesus "gave them power and authority to drive out all demons and to cure diseases." Power is the ability to do something; authority is the right to use that power. Jesus has both, and he delegated both to the Twelve. This foreshadows the promise of power and authority he would later give them in Matthew 28:19.

Jesus also gave his disciples instructions. First, he told them to travel light: "Take nothing for the journey—no staff, no bag, no bread, no money, no extra shirt." Obviously, the less you take, the faster you can go. But more significantly, this was designed to be a faith-building experience. They were going to go out empty-handed, trusting God to provide for their needs.

Jesus' second instruction was, "Whatever house you enter, stay there until you leave that town." Matthew expands on this instruction, saying, "Whatever town or village you enter, search there for some worthy person and stay at their house until you leave." "Worthy" describes someone who is spiritually open and sensitive—a person who would receive the good news the Twelve would be sharing. In Luke 10, Jesus described this desired host as a "man of peace." Having identified the household of a worthy person of peace, they were to remain there until they left the village.

Jesus also trained his disciples for the task he would assign them.

Jesus' third instruction was, "If people do not welcome you, leave their town and shake the dust off your feet as a testimony against them." Sadly, the gospel will not be accepted by everyone. We see that in the Parable of the Sower—not every heart is prepared to receive the good news.

Preach and heal; travel light; stay with a person of peace; leave if they won't receive you. I imagine the disciples had many questions and some fears, but this was enough to get them going, and that's what they did: "they set out and went from village to village, proclaiming the good news and healing people everywhere."

Luke tells us that "when the apostles returned, they reported to Jesus what they had done." No doubt they had a faith-building experience that was excellent training for the great task that they would later be given to do.

The Seventy-Two

A short time after the Twelve returned, Jesus sent out a larger group of seventy-two followers to "every town and place where he was about to go" (Luke 10:1–23). He now wanted to show the disciples that the mission—and his promise of power and authority—was not just for the twelve apostles.

This time, Jesus instructed the seventy-two to divide into pairs—he "sent them two by two." He also instructed them to pray. Jesus said, "The harvest is plentiful, but the workers are few. Ask the Lord of the harvest, therefore, to send out workers into his harvest field." He knew that the need is far greater than just seventy-two disciples could address. They were the first wave, but many, many more—millions—would be needed to get to every people and every place.

Finally, Jesus warned, "I am sending you out like lambs among wolves," acknowledging that the journey could be dangerous.

Still Today

Much of what Jesus commanded is still being practiced today. I know of one South Asian ministry that has engaged many people groups for the first time with the gospel. They go two by two, prayer-walking in a new place until the Holy Spirit identifies a person of peace. They then engage with that person, who invites them into their home, where they share the gospel and proclaim the coming of the Kingdom of God. Often that person becomes the first follower of Jesus in that place.

Nearly always their ministry is accompanied by healing and deliverance. The work is not always easy, and they have faced significant persecution and danger—they are like sheep among wolves. And sometimes they're required to move on from a place that will not receive them. But they have seen many people groups brought into the kingdom using the same model Jesus taught in Luke 9 and 10.

Visiting Caesarea Philippi

Caesarea Philippi, nestled at the foot of Mount Hermon, was a focal point of pagan worship in New Testament times, home to numerous shrines and temples dedicated to deities like Pan and Zeus. Herod the Great built a temple there to honor Caesar Augustus, and his son, Herod Philip, later expanded the city, renaming it Caesarea Philippi. It was a thoroughly Gentile city right on the edge of religious Galilee.

Matthew 16:13 says, "When Jesus came to the region of Caesarea Philippi," almost as if the visit was accidental. But Caesarea Philippi was not a place a devout Jew would casually visit, so Jesus must have intentionally planned a trip to this city. He knew the disciples would later go to many such pagan cities—places like Corinth, Ephesus, and even Rome—and he wanted to be with them on their first trip to such a place.

> Jesus knew the disciples would later go to many pagan cities, and he wanted to be with them on their first trip to such a place.

I imagine the disciples were shocked and disgusted by the things they saw in this pagan city. I wonder if they even questioned why Jesus would bring them to such a place.

While they were there, two remarkable things occurred. First, this is where Simon spoke the great confession: "You are the Messiah, the Son of the living God." Jesus affirmed that answer, saying, "Blessed are you, Simon son of Jonah, for this was not revealed to you by flesh and blood, but by my Father in heaven." He then declared, "And I tell you that you are Peter, and on this rock I will build my church, and the gates of Hades will not overcome it" (Matthew 16:16–18).

Interestingly, "the gates of Hades" is the name of a large cave at the foot of Mount Hermon, which the local population associated with the Greek god Pan. This cave contains a deep spring that was thought to be a bottomless abyss and an entrance to the underworld, or Hades—a portal to the realm of the dead. When I visited the place, our guide informed us it was a site for infant sacrifice in biblical times.

So when Jesus declared, "on this rock I will build my church, and the gates of Hades will not prevail against it," part of what he was saying is that Caesarea Philippi—and all the similar pagan strongholds of the world—would not be able to resist the coming of his kingdom. In effect, he proclaimed, "See all of this? The paganism? The immorality? The depravity? My church will conquer it all, here and everywhere else in the world."

This moment must have stayed with the disciples for the rest of their lives, strengthening and encouraging them as they took the gospel to pagan places around the world. Even today, Jesus' promise of victory over the forces of darkness and evil empowers his people as they work to see the Great Commission completed.

CONCLUSION

Jesus didn't just commission his followers to reach the nations— he prepared them to do so. Jesus modeled and taught a kingdom without boundaries. He also trained his followers through carefully planned lessons and encounters. As we look back on these early lessons, we see not only a call to "go" but a promise: Jesus is with us every step of the way, leading us across every barrier to reach a world he loves with the good news.

CHAPTER 4

The Start

Immediately after Jesus ascended into heaven, the small group of his followers remained in Jerusalem. They laid low, following Jesus' orders to wait for "the gift my Father promised . . . the Holy Spirit" (Acts 1:4–5).

After a few days, their obedience was rewarded. On Pentecost, "All of them were filled with the Holy Spirit and began to speak in other tongues as the Spirit enabled them" (Acts 2:4). Suddenly equipped and emboldened, Peter delivered the first gospel message. Three thousand who heard Peter's sermon were added to the church.

Acts 2:5 specifically mentions that "Jews from every nation under heaven" were present that day. So this was not a cross-cultural crowd—but it was geographically diverse, hailing from Rome, Egypt, Libya, Crete, and other parts of the Mediterranean world. Right off, Jesus' command about "the ends of the earth" was being accomplished.

Many of these new converts remained in Jerusalem for some time after the festival and joined the original church there. Others likely returned to their homes and were instrumental in establishing Christian communities in those places.

THE GREAT SCATTERING

Acts 3 through 7 describe the joys and difficulties of the first church in Jerusalem. One thing you won't find in those chapters is any evidence of "going." Jesus had commanded his people to go, but they were content to stay and enjoy the amazing blessings of the Jerusalem church.

So Jesus scattered them. Acts 6 and 7 tell about the martyrdom of Stephen, one of the first deacons of the Jerusalem church. And Acts 8 begins, "On that day a great persecution broke out against the church in Jerusalem, and all except the apostles were scattered throughout Judea and Samaria." According to Acts 11:19, "Those who had been scattered . . . traveled as far as Phoenicia, Cyprus and Antioch." In doing so, they (reluctantly) helped fulfill Jesus' command to take his good news to "all Judea and Samaria" and beyond.

The disciples had no clue how big the task was or how long it would take. Nevertheless, they set out to see it done.

The scattering of the early church is an example of an involuntary going, when God forces his people to leave the comfort of home and go to places where the good news is not yet known. We'll consider involuntary going in more depth in chapter 9.

PHILIP IN SAMARIA

One of those scattered was Philip, another of the original deacons in the Jerusalem church. According to Acts 8 he went to Samaria, to an unnamed city where he "proclaimed the Messiah." According to verses 6 through 8, "When the crowds heard Philip and saw the signs he performed, they all paid close attention to what he said. For with shrieks, impure spirits came out of many, and many who were paralyzed or lame were healed. So there was great joy in that city."

This is the first place in Acts where God validated the testimony of one of his messengers through "signs." It wouldn't be the last. Even today, in remote places around the world, the coming of the gospel is often accompanied by healings, demonic deliverances, and other miracles. These signs validate the messenger and his or her words so that people are more willing to listen and accept their message.

This is also the first clear instance in Acts of non-Jews coming to faith in Christ. The Samaritans were a mixed-race *ethnos*, who lived in the land between Judea and Galilee. The Jews despised their syncretic religious beliefs and scorned their mixed-race lineage. They avoided contact with Samaritans as much as possible. But Jesus had specifically mentioned Samaria as a place where the church should go, and so Philip put aside his prejudice and took the good news there. Undoubtedly, he had heard the story of the woman at the well and Jesus' own missionary work among this people.

When the apostles heard what was happening, they struggled to accept that anyone other than Jews could be Jesus followers. So Peter and John took a trip up to Samaria to see what Philip

The scattering of the early church is an example of an involuntary going.

was doing. When they arrived, they "prayed for the new believers there that they might receive the Holy Spirit" and "placed their hands on them, and they received the Holy Spirit" (Acts 8:15–17). Later, on their way home to Jerusalem, Peter and John "preach[ed] the gospel in many Samaritan villages" (Acts 8:25).

THE ETHIOPIAN EUNUCH

Accepting Samaritans into the kingdom was one thing—at least they had a historical connection to Israel, and Jesus himself had ministered among them. But God had much bigger things in mind.

So some time after Philip's Samaritan mission, the Holy Spirit instructed him to "go south to the road—the desert road—that goes down from Jerusalem to Gaza." Philip obeyed and along the way encountered "an important official in charge of all the treasury" of the queen of Ethiopia. This Ethiopian eunuch was headed home after a visit to Jerusalem. He was reading the scroll of Isaiah—the passage that begins "He was led like a sheep to the slaughter." Philip approached his chariot and asked the man, "Do you understand what you are reading?" When the official invited Philip to join him, Philip "began with that very passage of Scripture and told him the good news about Jesus." The man believed and asked, "Look, here is water. What can stand in the way of my being baptized?" (Acts 8:26–36).

Actually, several things might have stood in the way. For one, did Philip have the authority to baptize him, or was that task only for the apostles? Even today, in some parts of the world, baptism is reserved for bishops and other high officials of the church and cannot be performed by ordinary believers. This can be a hindrance to the spread of the church.

Another potential obstacle was that this man was an Ethiopian, and although he was at least a seeker, we don't know that he was a convert to Judaism. Was it OK to baptize a Gentile? Did he have to be circumcised first? Despite all that Jesus had taught and modeled, this would be a tough call for the early church for some time.

Third, this man was a eunuch, and according to Deuteronomy 23:1, eunuchs were excluded from the assembly of the Lord in Israel. Did that law also apply to the church? Could this man be baptized and welcomed into Christian fellowship?

Thankfully, Philip answered these questions liberally. Led by the Holy Spirit, he dismissed the obstacles and he "and the eunuch went down into the water and Philip baptized him" (Acts 8:38).

We don't have a biblical account about what happened to this man. But tradition says that he returned home as a near-culture missionary and began to spread the good news, laying the groundwork for one of the oldest Christian communities in the world.

PETER AND CORNELIUS

Acts 10 tells us about a man named Cornelius, a Roman centurion who lived in the coastal city of Caesarea. He was a good man, generous and devout. One day he had a vision of an angel who instructed him to send for a "man named Simon who is called Peter," which he did.

At about that same time, Peter had a vision of his own. God told him, three times, "Do not call anything impure that God has made clean" (Acts 10:15). The vision was about food, but God wanted Peter to understand that *people* were not to be regarded as unclean, no matter who they were or what they ate.

When Cornelius' men arrived, Peter welcomed the Gentile visitors into the house—something unheard of for a Jew. And the next day Peter, along with some Jewish believers, traveled to Cornelius' home, where after some initial awkwardness he declared a revolutionary truth: "I now realize how true it is that God does not show favoritism but accepts from every nation the one who fears him and does what is right" (Acts 10:34–35).

We can easily gloss over this sentence, but don't miss how powerful it is. As a Jew, Peter would have taken it for granted that God *did* show favoritism. Isn't that what the whole "chosen people" thing was about—that God *had* favored the Jews over every other *ethnos*? And yet there he was confessing just the opposite. This was a breakthrough for the early church, shattering the barriers between Jew and Gentile.

As Peter preached the gospel to this Gentile congregation, the Holy Spirit came upon them. Realizing the significance of this event, Peter baptized Cornelius, along with his friends and relatives, opening God's Kingdom to the Gentiles. The gospel had come to the Romans.

When Peter returned to Jerusalem, he faced sharp questions from the Jewish leaders of the Jerusalem church. Peter retold the story and concluded by saying, "If God gave them the same gift he gave us who believed in the Lord Jesus Christ, who was I to think that I could stand in God's way?" (Acts 11:17). The leaders of the church were satisfied: "So then, even to Gentiles God has granted repentance that leads to life" (Acts 11:18).

THE CHURCH AT ANTIOCH

By the end of Acts 11, there was a thriving Gentile church in the city of Syrian Antioch, 300 miles north of Jerusalem. When news of this Gentile movement reached Jerusalem, the church sent Barnabas to check it out. He was delighted by what he saw and stayed to pastor the church. When he needed help, he recruited Saul. Luke tells us that "for a whole year Barnabas and Saul met with the church and taught great numbers of people" (Acts 11:26).

This was the beginning of the first missionary journey.

In Acts 13 we read that "the Holy Spirit said, 'Set apart for me Barnabas and Saul for the work to which I have called them.' So after they had fasted and prayed, they placed their hands on them and sent them off" (Acts 13:2–3). This was the beginning of the first missionary journey—a primarily Gentile church sending out two of its pastors to unreached peoples and places. Which takes us to the most significant missionary figure in the New Testament.

THE APOSTLE PAUL

The apostle Paul pioneered cross-cultural missions. He was the first to intentionally go with the gospel to far-away places, the first to focus on Gentiles, and the first to share the gospel with them in culturally relevant ways. He was a strong advocate for a multi-ethnic Kingdom of God, insisting that people could follow Jesus without adopting Jewish customs.

Paul's missionary journeys are the first major example of obedience to Jesus' command to go. His three known missionary journeys took the gospel for the first time beyond the Middle East into Asia (modern-day Turkey), Macedonia and Achaea (Greece), and Europe. As a result, churches were planted in at least thirteen cities, including Corinth, Ephesus, and Athens. As Paul said of himself, he "fully proclaimed the gospel" "from Jerusalem all the way around to Illyricum" (modern Albania, Montenegro, and Croatia) (Romans 15:19). Many believe he later made a fourth, undocumented journey to Spain.

Paul was driven to reach those who had never heard and to expand the boundaries of God's Kingdom.

Paul was driven to reach those who had never heard and to expand the boundaries of God's Kingdom. He expressed his relentless commitment to going in his letter to the Romans: "It has always been my ambition to preach the gospel where Christ was not known" (Romans 15:20).

Paul's pattern was to begin in each place by preaching to the Jews, but his primary mission was to the Gentiles—he is called "apostle to the Gentiles" five times in the New Testament. This was no small task. The cultural and religious divide between Jews and

Gentiles was vast, and many vigorously resisted Paul's message. But Paul believed that Christ was for *every* nation, and his passion to bring the gospel to unreached peoples and places kicked off a global missionary movement that continues to this day.

Church Planting and Discipleship

As Paul traveled the world, he didn't just preach and move on. In each place he established churches and appointed leaders who would shepherd and oversee the flock. Jesus had commanded his people to "make disciples"; Paul accomplished that by planting churches. His commitment to discipleship through church planting ensured that those he evangelized would grow in their faith and be equipped to spread the gospel to others. This model of discipleship and church planting became the foundation for future missionary movements.

Paul also personally modeled what it meant to live as a Christian, saying, "Follow my example, as I follow the example of Christ" (1 Corinthians 11:1). Modern missionaries still carry this responsibility of modeling Christ-like living, and it can make all the difference. I know of one missionary to an Asian country who was arrested and charged with espionage and sedition. The authorities had access to his digital trail. What they found—his faithfulness to his wife and abstinence from pornography and profanity—convinced them he was not a threat but a man of genuine faith and character. Miraculously, they released him to continue his work.

Movement

Paul's third missionary journey focused on strengthening the churches he had already planted. He spent three years in Ephesus where, through Paul's daily teaching and the extraordinary miracles God was performing, a gospel movement was sparked. According to Acts 19:10, as a result "all the Jews and Greeks who lived in the province of Asia heard the word of the Lord." This is the goal of modern church-planting and disciple-making efforts: a Spirit-driven movement that touches every person in a region.

> The Jerusalem Council opened the door for the gospel to reach all nations.

Advocacy for the Gentiles

Paul's theology centered on salvation by grace through faith in Christ Jesus. This was good news for the Gentiles and opened the door for people from different cultures to receive Christianity. But it created conflict with Jewish Christians who insisted that Gentile converts observe Jewish customs, especially circumcision.

This conflict flared in a meeting between Paul and Peter (Galatians 2:11–14), where Paul rebuked Peter for his hypocrisy and defended the gospel of grace.

This same issue came to a head at the Jerusalem Council (Acts 15). Paul and Barnabas argued that Gentile believers should not be subject to the Mosaic Law. After much debate, the Council accepted their argument. That momentous decision opened the door for the gospel to reach all nations by allowing people groups to retain their cultural identity while joining the body of Christ.

Miracles

Everywhere he went, Paul's ministry was accompanied by signs and wonders that validated his message and demonstrated the power of God. In Lystra, for example, he healed a man crippled from birth (Acts 14:8–10). In Ephesus, even his handkerchiefs brought healing (Acts 19).

Today, many frontier missionaries report similar supernatural experiences—healings, dreams, deliverances—that demonstrate God's power. I've heard many say they couldn't do what they do without the Holy Spirit showing up in miraculous ways.

Language

In the first century, much of the world had been connected by a common language—Greek—and the prevalence of this shared language accelerated the spread of the gospel. Wherever Paul went, he was able to communicate in Greek rather than being required to learn a new local language or speak through a translator. When he wrote to the churches, he could do so in Greek, meaning that his letters were accessible everywhere in the Roman world.

This shared language strategy is still used today. In many places, missionaries use trade languages or national languages to make initial gospel connections with new people groups. We'll talk more about that in chapters 6 and 7.

Culture

Paul was uniquely equipped for cross-cultural ministry. As a devout Jew but also a Roman citizen, he understood both the Jewish and

Gentile worlds. That dual identity allowed him to adapt his message to different audiences while remaining faithful to the gospel. This is what he meant when he said, "I have become all things to all people so that by all possible means I might save some" (1 Corinthians 9:22).

We see this perhaps most vividly in Acts 17, where Paul speaks to the Areopagus, a prestigious body of philosophers and cultural leaders in Athens. Rather than quoting Scripture, he references an altar "to an unknown God" and even quotes a Greek poet. From there, he builds a bridge to the gospel and the resurrection. It was only because of his education that he would have known that poet and only because of his cultural sensitivity that he thought to build his presentation around that obscure altar.

> Paul's approach is still the foundation for cross-cultural missionary work today.

Paul's approach—faithful to the gospel but flexible in presentation—is still the foundation for cross-cultural missionary work today.

THE OTHER APOSTLES

Let's wrap up this chapter by considering how the other apostles fulfilled Jesus Great Commission. They were the ones who received the Great Commission directly from Jesus—what did they do in response? As shown in Table 1, most of them went out from Judea with the good news—some to very remote places like India and possibly Britain. All but one are thought to have died as martyrs.

Table 1. The Apostles' Mission Fields and Deaths

Apostle	Mission Field	How He Died
Peter	Jerusalem, Judea, Samaria, Rome	Crucified in Rome under Nero
Andrew	Scythia (Ukraine), Greece, Asia Minor	Crucified in Patras, Greece
John	Ephesus/Asia Minor	Died of old age in Ephesus
James	Jerusalem, Judea	Executed by Herod Agrippa I
Philip	Phrygia and Hierapolis (modern Turkey)	Martyred, possibly crucified or stoned
Bartholomew (Nathanael)	Armenia, Mesopotamia, possibly Persia and India	Possibly flayed or beheaded in Armenia
Matthew	Judea, Ethiopia, Persia, possibly India	Martyred in Ethiopia?
Thomas	Persia, India	Speared to death near Mylapore, India
James the Less	Possibly Egypt	Martyred in Egypt?
Thaddeus (Jude)	Mesopotamia, Syria, possibly Persia	Martyred in Syria or Persia
Simon the Zealot	Egypt, North Africa, possibly Persia or Britain	Martyred in Persia or Britain?
Matthias	Judea, possibly Ethiopia or Georgia	Martyred?

Even though the details are shrouded by time, it should be evident that the Twelve took the "every nation, every language, every place" commands seriously. They had no chance of completing the task, but nevertheless set out to see it begun. And they set the stage for future generations to continue the work—which is where we'll turn in the next chapter.

CHAPTER 5

The Race

After the deaths of the apostles, the gospel continued to spread—and it has continued to spread right down to the present day. For 2,000 years, God's people have been straining toward the "every nation, every language, every place" Great Commission finish lines. Sometimes the work has moved quickly, sometimes it has barely advanced at all, but by God's grace it has always moved forward.

In this chapter we'll take a whirlwind tour through the history of the Great Commission. My hope is that this history will give you a glimpse of how God has worked through the centuries and help you understand the foundation underlying today's work. But if you prefer, you can skip ahead to the next chapter, where we'll talk about the effort to reach the last few people groups with the gospel in this generation.

ROME

In the second and third centuries, Christians faced widespread persecution under a succession of Roman emperors. Yet persecution often fueled the spread of the gospel instead of suppressing it—a pattern that has held throughout history. Christianity continued to expand throughout the Roman Empire, from North Africa to Asia Minor and into parts of Europe. Early apologists like Justin Martyr and Tertullian defended the faith against Roman accusations and presented Christianity as a rational and moral religion. Over time, Christian communities grew, often in secret, but always committed to spreading the message of Christ.

During this time, catastrophic plagues ravaged the Roman Empire. The twenty-five-year Antonine plague may have claimed 25 percent of the empire's population, and at the height of the plague of Cyprian, thousands in Rome died every day.

For 2000 years, God's people have been straining toward the "every nation, every language, every place" finish lines.

Amidst these horrors, Christians stood out by caring for the sick and dying, even when others fled and even to the point of their own deaths. Their selfless acts of compassion saved lives and demonstrated the love of Christ in action, drawing many to the faith. Over time, such acts contributed to the empire's growing embrace of Christianity, culminating in Emperor Constantine's momentous conversion in 312 AD.[1]

Constantine's Edict of Milan in 313 AD legalized Christianity, ending centuries of oppression and allowing the faith to exist openly for the first time. Constantine's influence led to the Council of Nicaea in 325, which not only codified Christian doctrine but also brought about a unified church. This unity provided a secure platform for the gospel to spread throughout the empire.[2] But there was little "going" beyond that. And while the formal embrace of Christianity by Rome was good for Roman Christians, it alienated Rome's enemies, who saw Christianity as exclusively Roman.[3]

The invasions of Rome by the Goths and the Vandals in the fifth century led to the collapse of the Western Roman Empire. This created a power vacuum that allowed the church to take on a more central role in maintaining social order. Over time, the church's influence expanded, laying the foundation for the spread of Christianity into more remote parts of Europe.[4]

THE CELTIC CHURCH (400-900)

As the Roman Empire declined in the West, a new missionary force emerged from an unexpected place: Ireland. The Celtic church was established by Patrick, a Roman English missionary who founded churches, established monasteries, and trained leaders among the pagan Irish. Patrick wisely did not impose Roman culture on the Irish but—following the model of Paul—contextualized the message of Christ for them. Over time, Ireland became a bastion of the Christian faith, producing missionaries who would continue Patrick's work throughout the British Isles and Europe.[5]

THE VIKINGS (793-1066)

The Viking invasions of Europe, beginning in the late eighth century, were brutal and relentless. The seafaring Norsemen terrorized much of Europe with raids, destroying churches and monasteries and enslaving Christian populations.

THE SPRINT TO THE FINISH

PATRICK

Born into a Christian family in Britain around 385 AD, Patrick was kidnapped by Irish raiders at the age of sixteen and sold into slavery. For six long years, Patrick worked as a shepherd in the hills of Ireland, where he turned to God in his loneliness and desperation. One night, he had a dream in which he was told to escape. Obeying the vision, he fled 200 miles to the coast, found a boat, and returned to his homeland.

But that wasn't the end of his journey. After years of study in Gaul under the mentorship of Saint Germain of Auxerre, a prominent bishop, he had another vision—this time a call to return to Ireland, the land of his captors, and preach the gospel to the very people who enslaved him. Armed with nothing but the message of Christ, Patrick returned to a pagan Ireland to share the faith.

His mission was opposed by powerful forces. He often confronted the power of the druids and their pagan rituals, showing that the gospel was stronger than their magic. He also faced opposition from kings and chieftains who saw his message as a threat to their authority.

What followed was nothing short of miraculous. The gospel spread like wildfire, transforming Ireland into a Christian nation. Patrick baptized thousands, established churches, and even converted many local kings. His legacy turned Ireland into a center of Christian faith from which missionaries were sent out across Europe. What began with one man's obedience eventually sparked a movement that changed the world.

Yet in a surprising turn, the Vikings' frequent contact with Christian lands, through both trade and warfare, exposed them to the faith. Their prisoners—including women seized as slave wives—brought their faith with them into captivity. The Vikings saw that their victims' faith seemed unshakable, even under extreme duress.

Missionaries began to engage the Viking rulers, offering the gospel not as a foreign imposition but a transformative power that could strengthen their kingdoms. When important figures like King Harald Bluetooth of Denmark converted, it sparked a wave of Christianization across Scandinavia.

As the Vikings were drawn into Christianity, they themselves became carriers of the faith. Leaving behind their old ways of raiding and turning into protectors and spreaders of the gospel, they pushed the good news into new frontiers in the north.[6]

THE ERA OF CATHOLIC MISSIONS (500–1500)

In the medieval era, the Catholic Church became the dominant force in Christian missionary work. The collapse of the Roman Empire in the West led to a fragmented Europe, where pagan tribes like the Saxons, Franks, and Vikings still dominated. The Catholic Church, however, remained committed to the Great Commission.[7]

In the eighth century, Boniface led missions to convert the Germanic tribes. He established monasteries and dioceses, preaching the gospel and rooting out pagan practices. His work laid the foundation for Christianity in Germany, which would later become a stronghold of the faith.[8]

Another key moment came during the reign of Charlemagne. Crowned emperor of the Romans in 800, Charlemagne was

BONIFACE

Born in England around 675 AD, Boniface was a Benedictine monk. Called to bring the gospel to the pagan tribes of Germany, he left the safety of the monastery for the wild and hostile lands of northern Europe, knowing the dangers but trusting in God's power to transform hearts.

His most profound moment took place in the German village of Geismar. The people there worshipped Thor, the god of thunder, and believed his power was linked to the massive oak tree that stood in the center of the village: the Donar Oak. This tree was not just a symbol of their religion but a sacred site where sacrifices were offered. Boniface saw the tree as a barrier to their acceptance of the Christian faith.

In an act of profound courage and faith, Boniface resolved to demonstrate the superior power of the Christian God over the pagan deities by cutting down the oak. One day, he marched into the town square, took an ax, and began chopping. The people watched in shock, expecting lightning to strike Boniface dead on the spot. But nothing happened—the tree crashed to the ground, and with it, the power of their false god was shattered.

That was the turning point. Boniface used the lumber from the fallen oak to build a church, and many of the villagers turned to Christ. His courage to stand against paganism and preach the gospel without fear transformed entire regions. Boniface went on to plant churches, train leaders, and establish Christian communities across northern Europe.

deeply committed to expanding the Christian faith. Under his rule, missionaries were sent to the Saxons, Slavs, and other European tribes.[9]

Charlemagne's military conquests were often accompanied by efforts to Christianize the conquered peoples, sometimes by force, commencing a complicated relationship between political power and mission that would continue for centuries.[10]

During this period, Catholic monastic orders played a significant role in missions. The Benedictines emphasized both evangelism and education, helping to convert and civilize the pagan peoples of Europe. By establishing monasteries in newly converted regions, they provided stability and a long-term Christian presence. [11]

The Crusades (1096–1291) were primarily political and military endeavors, but they included some evangelistic efforts, such as Francis of Assisi's mission to Sultan al-Kamil in 1219. While the Crusades themselves were violent and ultimately unsuccessful, they had the unintended effect of expanding the European worldview and sparking further missionary zeal. Unfortunately, the Crusades also alienated the Muslim world from Christianity, which they associated—and often still do—with a militant, nationalistic form of Christianity.[12]

In the later medieval period, the Franciscan and Dominican orders emerged as powerful missionary forces. Franciscans, following the example of their founder, Francis of Assisi, focused on poverty and simplicity in their mission work. They traveled far beyond Europe, reaching North Africa and the Middle East. Dominicans concentrated on preaching and education to strengthen the faith in newly converted places.[13]

JOHN OF MONTECORVINO

John of Montecorvino was a Franciscan friar with a heart for the unreached. In 1291, he felt a call to bring the gospel to the Mongol Empire, a vast, remote realm ruled by the successors of Kublai Khan. Leaving the comfort of Europe, he embarked on a perilous journey, trusting God to open doors in a land where Christianity was unknown.

After years of travel, John arrived in Khanbaliq (modern Beijing) in 1294. For over a decade, he toiled alone, learning the language, building a humble church, and baptizing a few dozen souls amid scorn from rival Nestorian priests who branded him a heretic.

His breakthrough came in 1305. A young Mongol noble named Körgüz, son of an Ongut prince, had heard John's teachings and proposed a test: If his God was real, let him prove it by healing a crippled child. On a crisp autumn day, with the royal court assembled, John laid his hands on the child and prayed, calling on Christ's name. Moments later, the child rose, limping at first, then running to his mother's arms. Silence fell, then gasps rippled through the onlookers.

The miracle shattered Körgüz's doubts. He knelt before John, professing faith, and within weeks, hundreds followed. Over the next two years John baptized 6,000 new believers. His letter to Rome in 1307 glowed with joy: "The Lord has turned the hearts of this people." John's bold faith sparked a gospel flame in Asia, and as the first Archbishop of Khanbaliq, he nurtured a church that echoed Christ's power across the steppes.

THE AGE OF EXPLORATION (1500-1800)

By the end of the medieval period, Christianity had been established as the dominant faith across Europe but had not expanded much beyond that base. But the discovery of the Americas and the sea routes to Africa and Asia created unprecedented opportunities to pursue the Great Commission. Spanish and Portuguese explorers, backed by the Catholic Church, led the charge to bring the gospel to these far-flung lands.[14]

In the Americas, Catholic missionaries accompanied Spanish conquistadors. Bartolomé de las Casas evangelized indigenous peoples while advocating for their protection.[15] Junípero Serra brought the gospel to California, founding nine missions along the California coast over fifteen years. Missionaries established settlements and churches, particularly in Latin America, where the Catholic Church would eventually become deeply entrenched.[16]

By the end of the medieval period, Christianity had been established as the dominant faith across Europe, beyond that base.

Meanwhile, the Jesuits, founded in 1540 by Ignatius of Loyola, became an important missionary force. Francis Xavier, one of the original members of the Jesuit order, became legendary for his work in India, Japan, and China, where he pioneered the strategy of immersing himself in the language and culture of the people he evangelized.[17] In China, Matteo Ricci, another Jesuit, gained the respect of the Chinese imperial court by mastering their language and adopting their customs, while subtly introducing Christianity.[18]

During the same period, Catholic missionaries made significant inroads in Africa, particularly in Portuguese colonies.[19]

The Counter-Reformation, sparked by the Protestant Reformation in the sixteenth century, further revitalized Catholic missionary efforts. Catholic leaders saw the Great Commission as a means of countering Protestant influence by expanding the faith into newly discovered regions.[20]

THE REFORMATION (1500–1700)

In 1517, Martin Luther nailed his Ninety-Five Theses to the door of the Wittenburg Castle Church, sparking the Protestant Reformation. Interestingly, there was little emphasis on the Great Commission in the early days of the Reformation. Protestant leaders were more focused on reforming the church than on global evangelism. This inward focus continued for 200 years, during which little was accomplished toward the goal of reaching every people and every place.[21]

> There was little emphasis on the Great Commission in the early days of the Reformation.

THE MORAVIAN MISSION MOVEMENT (1727–1800)

The modern Protestant missionary movement began with the Moravians. Originally the followers of Jan Hus in fifteenth-century Bohemia, in the 1720s they found refuge from persecution in Herrnhut,

DAVID NITSCHMANN

David Nitschmann was one of the first missionaries to embrace Count Nicolaus Zinzendorf's vision to take the gospel to the ends of the earth.

Along with a fellow Moravian, Johann Leonhard Dober, Nitschmann volunteered to go to the island of St. Thomas, where they intended to evangelize the enslaved Africans. They were so committed to their mission that they were willing to sell themselves into slavery, if necessary, to reach the people they were called to serve.

Although they didn't become slaves, Nitschmann and Dober did go to St. Thomas. On their way, they nearly died in a severe storm at sea, which they interpreted as confirmation of God's call to endure hardship for the gospel. When they arrived, they had no money and no support from the colonial authorities. They lived and worked among the Africans, learning their languages and cultures, establishing personal relationships, and sharing the good news. Despite horrible living conditions and the hostility of plantation owners, Nitschmann persevered, and many came to Christ.

His efforts laid the groundwork for future missionary endeavors in the Caribbean. Nitschmann later became the first bishop of the Moravian Church and continued to support the mission work that spread across the globe, from Greenland to Africa and beyond.

Germany, under the protection of Count Nicolaus Zinzendorf. In 1727, a remarkable revival sparked a missionary movement that soon sent laborers to the unreached across the world.

The Moravians were driven by an intense dedication to fulfilling the Great Commission. Their motto, "May the Lamb that was slain receive the reward of His suffering," captured their passion for spreading the gospel.[22] The movement was energized by a twenty-four-hour prayer watch that endured for over a century. By the 1730s, Moravian missionaries were being sent to some of the most remote and difficult places in the world, including the Caribbean, North America, Africa, and Greenland.[23]

One of the Moravians' most impressive attributes was their willingness to go wherever the gospel was needed, even at great personal cost. Their radical commitment inspired not only those they ministered to but also the broader Protestant missionary movement. They influenced figures like John Wesley, the founder of Methodism, who experienced his spiritual awakening after encountering Moravian missionaries on a voyage to America.[24]

By the end of the eighteenth century, the Moravian Church had established hundreds of mission stations around the world, from the Arctic Circle to South America, laying the groundwork for the great missionary movements of the nineteenth century.[25]

THE PROTESTANT MISSIONARY REVIVAL (1800–1900)

The nineteenth century saw a revival of missionary zeal and an explosion of missionary work across the Protestant world. This period is known as the Great Century of Christian missions[26]—although I'd argue that the twentieth and twenty-first have been

SAMUEL ZWEMER

One of the most remarkable missionaries to emerge from the Student Volunteer Movement (SVM) was Samuel Zwemer, known as the Apostle to Islam. Zwemer was inspired by SVM's call to "evangelize the world in this generation" and dedicated his life to missionary work among Muslim populations, an effort that became one of the most challenging and impactful in modern missions.

Zwemer joined the SVM during his college years, moved by the lack of Christian missions in the Muslim world. In 1890, along with a few colleagues, he cofounded the American Arabian Mission, setting his sights on reaching the Arabian Peninsula. Zwemer and his wife, Amy Wilkes, spent decades in Bahrain, Iraq, and Egypt, sharing the gospel in regions often hostile to Christian missionaries.

Despite numerous hardships, including the death of two children, Zwemer's commitment never wavered. He worked tirelessly, not only as a missionary but also as a scholar and writer, producing numerous books and articles on Islam and Christian missions. His respectful approach to Islam earned him the opportunity to engage in deep conversations with Muslim scholars, though he saw only a few converts in his lifetime.

Zwemer's influence extended far beyond his personal efforts. His writings, leadership, and speaking engagements inspired a new generation of missionaries to enter the Muslim world. Today, his work remains foundational in the field of Christian missions to Islamic nations.

A. W. MILNE

When A. W. Milne, a missionary from the London Missionary Society, set out for the New Hebrides in 1829, he packed all his belongings in a coffin–a powerful symbol of his willingness to lay down his life for the gospel. Milne was well aware of the dangers, knowing that many missionaries before him had been martyred by the peoples of the islands. Despite the risks, he felt a deep call to go, fully accepting the possibility that he might never return.

Milne spent thirty-five years faithfully serving the people of the New Hebrides, sharing the message of Christ and ministering to the community. His dedication bore much fruit, and by the time of his death, he had witnessed a profound transformation among the people. In a remarkable tribute to his impact, the locals buried him in the center of their village, honoring him with this inscription: "When he came, there was no light. When he left, there was no darkness."

Milne's life of sacrifice and unwavering devotion has inspired generations of missionaries, symbolizing a deep dedication to the Great Commission.

even more impactful. If the pace of the Great Commission race had slowed to a walk in the previous centuries, it accelerated to a run during the 1800s.

The British missionary movement was at the forefront of this revival, largely due to the efforts of William Carey, often called the "father of modern missions." Carey, a British Baptist, sailed to India in 1793 and spent the next forty years preaching the gospel, translating the Bible into several Indian languages, and founding schools and hospitals. His famous saying, "Expect great things from God; attempt great things for God," inspired a generation of missionaries. Carey's work led to the founding of the Baptist Missionary Society, which became one of the key organizations in the global mission movement.[27] The missionary awakening in

The 19th century is often referred to as the Great Century of Christian missions.

Britain spread rapidly. The London Missionary Society (LMS), established in 1795, sent missionaries to Africa, the Pacific Islands, and China. LMS missionary Robert Morrison became the first Protestant missionary to China in 1807, translating the Bible into Chinese and opening the door for future missionary work in Asia. [28] A. W. Milne, another LMS missionary, was the first to go to the New Hebrides (now Vanuatu) [29].

Hudson Taylor, another Englishman, pioneered a revolutionary approach to missions in China. He famously refused to ask for money to support his work and instead relied solely on prayer for God's provision. When he went to China in 1854, he immersed himself in Chinese culture, emulating Paul's model of becoming "all things to all people so that by all possible means I might save some" (1 Corinthians 9:22).[30]

American missionaries were also instrumental in spreading the gospel throughout Asia, the Middle East, and Africa. The Haystack

JIM AND ELISABETH ELLIOT

Jim Elliot was an American missionary whose life and death made a profound impact on Christian missions. While studying at Wheaton College in the late 1940s, he became convinced of the need to take the gospel to unreached people groups.

Elliot and his wife, Elisabeth, joined a missionary team in Ecuador, where they worked to reach the Waorani (also known as Auca), an isolated and often hostile indigenous tribe. Along with four other missionaries—including pilot Nate Saint—Elliot set out to contact the Waorani in 1955. They used a small plane to fly over Waorani territory, dropping gifts and calling out friendly messages in their language.

After months of preparation, the team landed near the Waorani village on January 3, 1956. For several days, they made friendly contact with a few tribe members. However, on January 8, 1956, a group of warriors attacked the missionaries, spearing all five men to death.

But the story didn't end there. In an extraordinary act of grace, Elisabeth Elliot, Nate Saint's sister Rachel, and others later returned to live among the Waorani. Over time, they shared the message of Christ's love and forgiveness with the very people who had killed their loved ones.

Mincaye—the man who had killed Jim Elliot—was deeply impacted by their message of God's love for his enemies and gave his life to Christ. His life stands as a testament to the transformative power of the gospel and the incredible grace of those who chose to love their enemies.

Prayer Meeting, held in 1806 by five Williams College students, is widely regarded as the birth of the American foreign missions movement. It ignited a passion for global evangelism among American Christians and led to the formation of the American Board of Commissioners for Foreign Missions (ABCFM) in 1810.[31]

Perhaps the most famous American missionary of this period was Adoniram Judson. He sailed to Burma in 1813 and spent nearly forty years translating the Bible into Burmese and establishing numerous churches while enduring immense hardship, including the loss of two wives and seventeen horrific months' imprisonment.[32]

The Second Great Awakening in the United States (roughly 1795–1835) also contributed to the growing missionary spirit. Revivalist preachers like Charles Finney and movements such as the Student Volunteer Movement (SVM) energized thousands of young people to dedicate their lives to missionary service. The SVM, founded in 1886 by D. L. Moody, aimed to achieve "the evangelization of the world in this generation" and inspired many young people to go to the mission field.[33]

Women played a significant role in this missionary expansion. Figures like Lottie Moon, a Southern Baptist missionary in China, helped break cultural barriers, engaging in evangelistic work and social reforms.[34]

The exploration of Africa during the nineteenth century also opened new mission fields. David Livingstone, a Scottish missionary and explorer, combined evangelism with efforts to end the slave trade and improve living conditions for Africans.[35]

The nineteenth century also saw the emergence of the first indigenous missionary leaders, including Pandita Ramabai, a Hindu

AMY CARMICHAEL

Born in Ireland in 1867, Amy Carmichael grew up with a deep love for God and a heart for the needs of others. In 1893, she left for the mission field—never to return home. Her journey took her first to Japan, then briefly to China and Ceylon (modern-day Sri Lanka), before God called her to India, where she would serve faithfully for the next fifty-five years.

At first, Carmichael focused on language learning and open-air evangelism. She rejected Western dress and customs, choosing instead to live simply and fully identify with the Indian people she served.

Everything changed when she encountered the heartbreaking reality of children—especially young girls—being trafficked into Hindu temples and forced into ritual prostitution. Deeply moved, Amy began rescuing these children. With the help of local believers and fellow missionaries, she established a haven, the Dohnavur Fellowship in Tamil Nadu.

As the years passed, the work expanded. Amy and her team rescued hundreds of abandoned and exploited children, offering them not only food and shelter but also love, dignity, and a Christian education. Many came to faith and were baptized.

In 1931, a fall left her mostly bedridden. But she didn't stop working. From her room, she wrote dozens of books, devotionals, and poems—many of which still inspire readers with her faith, courage, and unwavering obedience to Christ.

convert, and Samuel Ajayi Crowther, a former slave.[36] This trend continued in the twentieth century and has accelerated in recent years. It is one reason we're rapidly approaching the Great Commission finish lines.

THE TWENTIETH CENTURY AND THE RISE OF GLOBAL MISSIONS (1900–2000)

At the dawn of the twentieth century, the global missionary movement was racing ahead. Christianity had expanded into every corner of the world, and new mission strategies emerged to meet the needs of a rapidly changing global landscape.

In 1910, the Edinburgh Missionary Conference brought together missionaries and leaders from across the Protestant world to discuss strategies for completing the Great Commission.[37]

Following the Azusa Street Revival in 1906, the Pentecostal mission movement grew rapidly. Pentecostal missionaries spread throughout the Americas, Africa, and Asia, planting churches and igniting revival movements.[38]

In Latin America, Africa, and Asia, the twentieth century was marked by the rapid expansion of evangelical and Pentecostal Christianity. In China, despite severe persecution under communist rule, the underground church grew exponentially. The efforts of nineteenth-century missionaries like Hudson Taylor laid a foundation that could survive the harshest conditions, and by the end of the century, as many as 100 million Chinese had come to faith in Christ.[39]

The Jesus Movement of the 1960s and 1970s also played a significant role in revitalizing missions, particularly among young people. Youth With A Mission (YWAM), founded by Loren

Cunningham in 1960, sent waves of young missionaries across the globe. YWAM grew rapidly, with bases in nearly every country by the end of the century.[40]

During the second half of the twentieth century, Billy Graham led massive crusades around the world, preaching to millions and inspiring many to become missionaries. His Lausanne Congress on World Evangelization in 1974 reaffirmed the urgency of the Great Commission and called for a renewed global effort to reach the unreached.[41] And his Amsterdam Conferences, especially Amsterdam 2000, brought together evangelists, pastors, and church leaders from more than 200 countries to equip them for gospel outreach.[42]

At the dawn of the twentieth century, the global missionary movement was racing ahead.

Amsterdam 2000 gave birth to Table 71—named for the table number where a group of key leaders sat during the conference—which focused attention on the world's remaining unengaged and unreached people groups. These leaders recognized the need for coordination and collaboration to reach the most remote and least evangelized places.

Table 71 likewise birthed Call2All, led by Mark Anderson, and Finishing the Task, originally led by Paul Eshelman. Through its annual conference and famous list of unengaged, unreached people groups, FTT called attention to the large number of people groups that still had not heard and accelerated the effort to engage those groups with the gospel. And that's where we'll pick up the story in chapter 6.

PART THREE

The Sprint

CHAPTER 6

Believers in Every Nation

From beginning to end—from Genesis to Revelation—God's Word declares his heart for the nations. In Genesis 22:18, God promises Abraham that "through your offspring *all nations on earth* will be blessed, because you have obeyed me." That's a promise that God's gift of salvation by grace through faith in Jesus Christ would be for every nation. In Revelation 7, John has a vision of "a great multitude that no one could count, from *every nation, tribe, people and language*, standing before the throne and before the Lamb" (Revelation 7:9).

These promises bookend Jesus' command, given to his disciples just before his ascension, to "go and make disciples of all nations"—the first of the three Great Commission finish lines. In this chapter we'll explore the effort to reach every nation on earth with the gospel.

WHAT IS A NATION?

When you hear the word *nation*, you probably think of a country—England, Indonesia, and so on. And for centuries, that's the way the church conceived of the "every nation" task. Missionaries went out from Europe and America to *countries* where the gospel was unknown. By the 1940s that work had succeeded in planting churches in many parts of most of these countries—so much so that many Christians and mission organizations were concluding that the Great Commission was effectively completed.[1]

From beginning to end—from Genesis to Revelation—God's Word declares his heart for the nations.

But about that same time, new thinking was emerging. Cameron Townsend, a Bible translator and later the founder of Wycliffe Bible Translators, was convicted when a Guatemalan Indian leader asked him, "If your God is so smart, why can't he speak my language?" He began calling attention to the many language groups worldwide that had no access to the gospel. In 1955, missiologist Donald McGavran published his book *Bridges of God*, which observed that the gospel tends to spread rapidly within a homogenous ethnic, social, or cultural group but slowly—if at all—across such barriers.[2]

This was the beginning of people-group missiology, which viewed the Great Commission task not as primarily geographical but ethnic and linguistic. According to this new idea, the "nations" of the Bible are not countries, but *people groups*, and the task of the Great Commission is to "make disciples" among every one of those groups. Dr. Ralph Winter, at the Lausanne Conference in 1974, famously called for a new era of cross-cultural missions aimed at launching an indigenous gospel movement in every people group.[3]

This new definition of "nations" matches the plain meaning of the Bible. In the New Testament—and in the Septuagint, the Greek Old Testament—"nation" is the Greek word *ethnos*, from which we get our English words *ethnic* and *ethnicity*. In the Bible, an *ethnos* is a group of people who share a common ethnicity, ancestry, heritage, culture, geography, and language—an ethnolinguistic people group. This is the word used in Matthew 28:19 to define the Great Commission task: "Go and make disciples of *pante te ethne*"—all the people groups.

THE ORIGIN OF THE NATIONS

Where did these nations come from? The Scriptures teach that God created them at Babel. According to Genesis 11, "The LORD came down to see the city and the tower the people were building" in disobedience to his earlier command to "fill the earth." So he "confuse[d] their language" and "scattered them from there over the whole earth." Before this time, "the whole world had one language and a common speech." There were no nations—the whole world was unified through a common language. But after this, they were divided and scattered.

Why did God do this? The obvious reason was to enforce his command that humankind "fill the earth." If the people would not spread out by themselves, God would scatter them. Second, though, God separated the nations to protect humankind. By dividing humanity, God limited what any one nation—or any one ruler—could accomplish, for good, but especially for evil. Third, the separation of the nations launched the proliferation of human cultures around the world. Human culture is astoundingly diverse.

As the gospel reaches different nations, each one brings their unique expressions of praise to God, magnifying his glory.

When the Bible says God scattered them, you can be sure he did it well. The world's people groups are distributed across six continents in just about every climate and environment. There are many in some places and few in others. The West African country of Nigeria—about the size of Texas—has over 450 people groups. India has several times that many. Other countries, like Sweden and France, historically were ethnically homogenous, with only a few small *ethne* obscured among the majority population. (As we'll see in chapter 9, that ethnic homogeneity has changed in recent years through massive immigration—another part of God's plan for reaching the world.)

> God not only scattered the nations, but He specifically determined where each one would live on the planet.

In many places, like the Caucuses Mountains and the Amazon, the people groups are geographically as well as culturally distinct, with each group isolated to a small region or just a few villages. In other places, like India, they are swirled together into an amazing collage of humanity. Both present challenges to Great Commission work.

By the way, according to Acts 17, God not only scattered the nations, but he specifically determined where each one would live on the planet. In Paul's sermon to the Areopagus, he says, "From one man he made all the nations, that they should inhabit the

THE GOROSE

Ethiopia has a Christian heritage that traces back to Bible times. Sadly, though, the country also has many people groups who have never heard the gospel.

Among those are the Gorose, an isolated group found in western Ethiopia. The Gorose are animists who worship and fear the spirits. As far as anyone knows, there has never been even one Gorose believer. In fact, there is no record of anyone ever going to the Gorose to tell them about Jesus.

But in early 2022, a team of missionaries led by an Ethiopian believer named Amasaganalu climbed the mountain to the Gorose villages. There they met the parents of a boy named Getenet, who had been paralyzed and mute for five years. His parents had taken him to the hospital and the witchdoctors, but nothing had worked. Desperate, they asked the missionaries to pray for their boy, and as they prayed in Jesus' name, God miraculously healed him, enabling him to speak and walk. The parents began to praise God and quickly gave their lives to Jesus. They became the first Gorose believers—ever!

As word of the healing spread, hundreds of Gorose received the gospel. Entirely on their own, many of the new believers brought their charms and fetishes to be burned as a sign of their commitment to Christ. Today there is a thriving, growing community of believers among the Gorose.

The Gospel has come to the Gorose!

whole earth; and he marked out their appointed times in history and the boundaries of their lands" (Acts 17:26). Why did God do this? "So that they would seek him and perhaps reach out for him and find him" (Acts 17:27). In other words, even in scattering the nations God had his Great Commission purpose in mind.

HOW MANY?

It is hard to know exactly how many biblical nations there are on earth. Any attempt to count them begins with assumptions and understandings that significantly affect the final count.

For example, should a people group be counted once in its place of origin or greatest population, or multiple times to account for its diaspora populations? The Han Chinese people group has subpopulations in most countries around the world. Are those separate people groups or are they all part of one big group? How about groups that are artificially divided by national boundaries? Should they be considered one group or several—one in each country? Similarly, how should the various combinations of language, culture, and caste be regarded in India and other South Asian countries? Is every combination a separate group?

Any attempt to count the nations begins with assumptions and understandings that significantly affect the final count.

Several excellent attempts have been undertaken to answer the "how many" question. Each has begun with different assumptions and arrived at a different answer. They overlap significantly, but they also differ in important ways, making it difficult to reconcile them. Nevertheless, these databases are useful tools for those who are committed to seeing the gospel taken to "every nation."

The Joshua Project is the data and research arm of Frontier Ventures, formerly the U.S. Center for World Mission, founded by Dr. Ralph Winter in 1976. At their website, Joshuaproject.org, you'll find detailed profiles of over 17,000 people groups, along with interactive maps, prayer guides, and mobilization tools. [4]

PeopleGroups.org is the public face of the data arm of the International Mission Board (IMB) of the Southern Baptist Convention. PeopleGroups.org offers data on over 12,000 people groups, including gospel status—reached, unreached, or unengaged.[5]

Finishing the Task (FTT) is a network of churches, mission organizations, and individuals formed by Table 71 to speed the completion of the Great Commission. While Joshua Project and PeopleGroups.org track the overall status of evangelization, FTT has been especially focused on unengaged, unreached people groups (UUPGs or, simply, unengaged groups)—those groups that have no known missionary or church presence.

Each month from 2005 to 2021, FTT published a list—adapted from the IMB's data—of the world's unengaged groups. CEO Paul Eshleman carried that list everywhere he went and shared it with anyone he thought might help with the task. Paul's advocacy probably did more than any other single thing to accelerate the effort to engage the unengaged groups. Sadly, that effort ended with the transition of FTT leadership after Paul's death, and the list has not been formally updated for some time.

However, FTT incubated the Finishing Fund, which since 2020 has carried on FTT's commitment to the unengaged. The Fund has continued to do its best to track the progress toward completing the FTT list of groups.

As we've said, the lists of people groups vary based on the assumptions that were made when they were created. In addition, the world is a big place and many parts of it are very hard to reach, making collecting and maintaining information about all these groups challenging. One thing we can be sure of is that none of the lists is perfect.

The bottom line is that only the Father knows exactly where the finish line lies. The good news is we don't have to guess—our job is to keep working until the day Jesus comes back to tell us that we've finished. I hope that won't be long.

REACHED, UNREACHED, AND UNENGAGED

The various people groups of the world can be divided into three tiers based on their level of gospel engagement. At the top are the reached groups, typically defined as those where greater than 2 percent of the population is Christian. In the reached world, there are many believers and churches, and the gospel is readily accessible. Not everyone in the reached world is a believer, but in the reached world the gospel is available to anyone who desires to hear it.

Virtually every people group in North America and Europe is in this tier.

Next are the unreached groups, those with Christian populations less than 2 percent but more than zero. There are thousands of people groups and billions of people in this category. An example would be the Turkish people. There are about 63 million people in the country of Turkey, and perhaps 0.02 percent of them—about 12,000—are Christians.[6] So while technically there is a Christian presence among the Turks, it is microscopic, and the typical Turk likely will never encounter a Turkish Christian during her life. The groups in this category remain a major focus of Great Commission activities, especially church planting, which we'll talk about in chapter 8.

At the bottom of the stack are the unengaged people groups (sometimes called unengaged unreached people groups, or UUPGs). These groups have no known Christian presence at all—no believers, no churches, and sadly no effort to engage them with the gospel. The people in these groups have never heard the name of Jesus—or know him only as a prophet of Islam—and have no access to the gospel.

The remaining unengaged groups are mostly very small and are found in remote, difficult, dangerous places.

As you might expect, the remaining unengaged groups are mostly very small—typically just a few thousand people—and are found in remote, difficult, dangerous places. Some live in countries that are closed to the gospel. Many are Muslim groups. Some are aggressively hostile to outsiders. Most are not literate. They are the last groups for a reason! But reaching them is the first finish line of the Great Commission race, a task that might well be accomplished in the next year or two.

GOD'S PLAN FOR THE NATIONS

Even though it was God who divided the nations, his plan has always been to unify them again under Jesus Christ through the gospel. In Ephesians 2:13–16, we read,

> But now in Christ Jesus you who once were far away have been brought near by the blood of Christ. For he himself is our peace, *who has made the two groups one* and has destroyed the barrier, the dividing wall of hostility, by setting aside in his flesh the law with its commands and regulations. *His purpose was to create in himself one new humanity out of the two*, thus making peace, and in one body to reconcile both of them to God through the cross, by which he put to death their hostility.

The two groups Paul was describing were Greeks and Jews, but these verses apply to every people group on earth. Just as God united the Jews and Greeks in Ephesus, he is also creating "one new humanity"—the church—that includes people from every *ethne*. And in that one body he is reconciling all of them "to God through the cross, by which he put to death their hostility."

God's plan has always been to unify them again under Jesus Christ through the gospel.

That is a remarkable claim—that through Jesus Christ, God plans to unify thousands of people groups and "put to death" the hostility that divides them. Many think we have a corner on racism here in the United States, but it's pretty much true that people everywhere hate and fear "the other." One day soon, God will bring tremendous glory to himself by putting an end to all that hatred and racism through Christ.

By the way, the world is constantly striving to accomplish this goal—the unification of the world's peoples—apart from God. That's the impulse behind world empires and the motivating force behind the modern utopian globalist movement. Ultimately, this desire will be briefly fulfilled, under the rule of the antichrist, during the Great Tribulation. But then God's authentic kingdom will come and sweep that false kingdom away.

WHERE DO WE STAND?

The church has been working for 2,000 years to fulfill the Great Commission, and much has been accomplished. But exactly where do we stand in the effort to make disciples of "all nations?"

As I've said, opinions differ about these numbers. My data is based on the work of Finishing the Task and my own firsthand knowledge gained as the managing partner of the Finishing Fund. Based on that, I can tell you that in 2005 the first FTT list showed about 3,500 unengaged groups, with a total population of over 700 million people. That's about 30 percent of the world's people groups where there was zero Christian presence.

But over the last few years the number of unengaged groups has declined dramatically. By 2017, the number was down to about 1,450 groups. In the eight years since, nearly every one of those groups—plus about 700 more that were added to the list in those years—have now been engaged with the gospel. All those groups now have active evangelistic and church-planting efforts underway, and most have believers and churches. As I write this in 2025, based on my best information, fewer than 100 groups remain unengaged. By God's grace I hope that by the time you read this, work will have begun in most of them.

Some of these remaining groups will be very tough to engage. One example is the Sentinelese people, a tiny group of about 50 souls who live on a small island in the Indian Ocean. Almost nothing is known about these people—including their language—because they are so aggressively hostile to outsiders. In 2018, a young American missionary named John Chau was killed when he tried to take the gospel to them. Efforts continue to reach these people with God's good news, but so far no one has been successful.

In fairness, not everyone agrees with my opinion about the remaining task. At the time of this writing, PeopleGroups.org says that there are 3,149 remaining unengaged groups.[6] That's an enormous difference—what's the explanation? Well, as I said, the answers you get when counting people groups depend a lot on the assumptions you make. If you're interested in learning more, you can turn to Appendix 1 for the details.

HOW DOES IT HAPPEN?

Engaging an unengaged people group requires intentionality. The remaining groups are small and remote and can be easily overlooked. Thankfully, the availability of the FTT list and other sources have raised the awareness of the world's missionary force about the opportunity to engage the remaining groups.

Different ministries use different approaches to engage people groups, but all involve sending a small team of trained indigenous

THE GREGH

The Gregh are a minority people group living in five villages in the remote mountains of a small central Asian country. In 2000 years, no one had ever gone to the Gregh with the gospel of Jesus Christ. To the best of anyone's knowledge, there had never been even one Gregh believer.

But in March 2018, after much prayer and fasting, a team of believers from that country made the treacherous journey over the mountains to one of the five Gregh villages. The team had asked God to lead them to a person of peace among the Gregh.

As they approached the village, they encountered a man named Abdul walking beside the road with his cattle. They stopped, engaged him in conversation, and began sharing the gospel. As Abdul heard the good news for the first time, he began to weep, confessing that he had been deeply troubled by his sin and had not known how to be free of his burden of guilt. On the spot, Abdul accepted God's gift of forgiveness. He became the first known Gregh believer—ever!

Abdul immediately invited the team to his house, where they shared the gospel with his family. They now know Jesus, and Abdul's home has become the site of the first Gregh church.

By God's grace the good news is spreading, bringing hope to a people who before only knew slavery to religious ritual, with no forgiveness, no peace, no assurance, and no freedom.

The gospel has come to the Gregh!

missionaries to the group. Some ministries use the simple model described in Luke 10. The team will go to the people group, praying for the Holy Spirit to identify a person of peace among them. They will then connect with that person and share the gospel. Often that person of peace will become the first believer in that place and his or her house the first church.

As I write this in 2025, based on my best information, fewer than 100 groups remain unengaged.

From there the gospel spreads through the person of peace's family and friends. Ideally, the missionaries remain in the people group, evangelizing, teaching, and training emerging leaders, for a period—at the Finishing Fund we say three years—at which point the church can stand on its own feet.

When the gospel first enters a new place, there will be only a single church: a handful of believers meeting in a home. Increasingly, though, church planters are using techniques like Discovery Bible Study that lead to rapid multiplication of churches and movements of church planting and disciple-making, where one church quickly reproduces into many daughter churches. When the Spirit begins a movement, the church can spread rapidly through a people group. We'll talk more about movement in chapter 8.

There are variations on this model. Some ministries use a simple business—a tea shop or tractor rental—as an entry strategy, especially among hostile groups. Others use a humanitarian ministry to get started. I know of two ministries—Mission India and GTi Hope—that have great success with literacy programs. Other

THE HALA

The Hala people are subsistence rice farmers who live in the remote mountain highlands of a Southeast Asian country. They are animists who worship their ancestors and believe in supernatural forces, including spirits of the forest, the water, and the mist.

As far as anyone knows, there has never been even one Christian among the Hala. In fact, there is no record of anyone ever having gone to the Hala with the gospel.

But in late 2020, a team of missionaries from that country visited the Hala for the first time and began telling them about Jesus. The people were resistant, telling those who showed interest, "If you believe in Christ, you must pay them money, and when you die, none of us will help your family."

One man, named Vinh, heard the gospel several times without responding. But when he was told that Jesus could heal, he asked, "Can God heal my eyes? They are very painful, and I cannot sleep. I went to the hospital many times, but the doctor could not help me." The believers asked, "Do you trust that God can heal you?" and he said, "I believe in God; please pray for me." The missionaries prayed for him and, by God's grace, he was able to sleep that night without any pain.

The next day, Vinh became the first Hala believer—ever! Two weeks later, his wife prayed to receive Christ, and they are now asking God to save their three sons and their families as well.

The gospel has come to the Hala!

ministries might offer a health clinic or undertake a water project to gain access to an otherwise resistant place.

Virtually all these new engagements are accomplished using a shared language. This works because people in most parts of the world are at least bilingual, speaking their own local language plus some regional language. Just as Paul used Greek to bridge language barriers in the first century, modern missionaries use this "shared language" approach when engaging a new people group. In India, the shared language might be Hindi; in East Africa, Swahili; in South America, Portuguese or Spanish. Almost always that's sufficient to begin evangelizing and establish the first churches.

But as the gospel spreads in a people group, new believers begin to desire the Scriptures in their own, local heart language. That's when the process of Bible translation usually begins. We'll look at that in the next chapter.

Many great ministries have contributed to the sprint toward the "every nation" finish line, but a few stand out in my mind: Team Expansion, which has done amazing work in Southeast Asia and South America; New Covenant Missions, which has engaged more than fifty groups across Africa; and Global Obedience, which has helped engage a number of East Asian groups.

WHY HAS IT HAPPENED?

Why has so much happened in such a short period of time? A major factor has been increased awareness, brought about by leaders like Paul Eshleman of FTT and Mark Anderson of Call2All. The world is much more aware of the problem and the opportunity of the unengaged than it was twenty-five years ago, and the missions community has stepped up to the challenge.

Another factor is good research, including the lists published by IMB and Joshua Project. For the first time in history, we know who and where all the world's *ethne* are.

Innovations in church planting and disciple making, especially among oral peoples, have also helped accelerate the work.

Another key, of course, is advances in technology: automobiles and motorbikes, airplanes, radio, TV, the Internet, and so on. People and information—including the good news—move much faster and further today than they ever have before.

A significant factor in the rapid progress over the last few years is the emergence of the indigenous church as a missionary force. All around the world, the local church is stepping up to the challenge of engaging the last unengaged

> *By far the most important reason for the rapid expansion of God's Kingdom into the unengaged groups is the powerful movement of the Holy Spirit.*

groups with the gospel. They are sending national missionaries who are culturally close to the unengaged and who share a language with them. These near-culture missionaries can take the gospel much more effectively and at much lower cost than Western missionaries.

A MOVEMENT OF THE SPIRIT

By far the most important reason for the rapid expansion of God's Kingdom into the unengaged groups is the powerful movement of the Holy Spirit. He is working around the world to gather in a great end-times harvest. We have all heard stories of missionaries in the old days who would give their whole lives to a place and see only a handful of converts. Today, the missionaries funded by the Finishing Fund often see the first new believer in an unengaged place within the first week—sometimes on the first day.

Miracles

One evidence of the Spirit's work is signs and wonders, which often accompany the arrival of the gospel in a new place. These include miraculous healings and demonic deliverances. This is consistent with what we see throughout the history of the church—God acts through his Spirit to validate the testimony of his people supernaturally.

There are so many stories! In one animistic people group in East Africa, a little boy who had been paralyzed and mute nearly from birth was fully healed. Hundreds in his formerly animistic people group now follow Jesus. In Nepal, a young man whose sister had accepted Christ was healed when she prayed for him. This led their parents and 50 others to become believers. In a high-caste Indian group, a man with back pain and two women with cancer were healed through the prayers of the missionary, bringing thirteen of their family and friends into God's Kingdom. Over and over, around the world, the Spirit is moving to demonstrate the power of the Living God.

While we in the West might be skeptical about such things, they make perfect sense to me. When a missionary enters a village in an unengaged place, bringing the gospel for the first time, in a spiritual sense it might as well be 50 AD. Why would the Spirit not do today what he did to validate the testimony of Paul and others in the first century? I am thankful that he does.

Dreams and Visions

Another way the Spirit is accelerating the work—especially among Muslims—is through dreams and visions. Typically, a person dreams of a man in blazing white clothes who says, "Follow me" (or something similar). Often the dreamer is overwhelmed by a sense of love. Sometimes he realizes that the vision is of Jesus; sometimes he doesn't—but wants to know more.

In every story I've heard, the man in the vision directs the dreamer to seek out a Christian. This is consistent with what we learned in chapter 1: that the Great Commission is our job.

My Finishing Fund partner Mark Haumschilt has encountered many Muslims who've had dreams and visions. He tells one story of an elderly Yazidi man in Iraq. The Yazidis are a persecuted minority people group in Iraq, with their own distinct syncretic faith. Mark met this man—the patriarch of his family—in a refugee camp. Through a translator, the man told of a dream where a man in a white robe warned him that he would be captured by ISIS, held, and later released. The man told Mark that everything the dream predicted had come true. Then he told Mark, "You were also in

> I believe the church is only a handful of years away from fulfilling Jesus' command to "go and make disciples of all nations."

111

THE FASHAWANA

The Fashawana are a small tribe who live in the Nuba Mountain region of Sudan—a region with many people groups and very few believers. Although the Fashawana are officially Sunni Muslims, many among the people group practice "folk Islam," weaving together Islamic beliefs and witchcraft. As far as anyone knows, there has never been a Christian among the Fashawana.

But recently two Sudanese believers—Ahmed and Kalo—went to the Fashawana and began telling people about Jesus.

One day Ahmed encountered a woman who was in agony. "I'm very, very sick and my body is all in pain!" she said. "Someone has put a curse on me, and their witchcraft has caused this disease in my body."

"I will pray for you," Ahmed said, "but first you need to believe in the Lord Jesus Christ. He is the one who can heal you. You need to leave your own magic and witchcraft. If you do that, I will pray for you, and you will be healed." She agreed, and he prayed for her.

Early the next morning, Ahmed returned to the woman's hut and met her family. Seizing the opportunity, he introduced the family to the Word of God. Then he prayed for the woman again. She had put her faith in Jesus and gained complete healing. Today she has is actively sharing her faith with the Fashawana community.

The gospel has come to the Fashawana!

my dream. And now you're here to tell us how to follow the man in white." Mark was surprised, but he quickly shared the gospel with the family, who all received Christ. They started a small house church, led by the son of the dreamer, which has since multiplied in the camp.

WHAT COMES NEXT?

I believe the church is only a handful of years away from fulfilling Jesus' command to "go and make disciples of all nations." Only about one hundred people groups remain that have not heard, and the push is on to see them engaged.

Engaging all the world's people groups with the gospel will be a significant accomplishment. Jesus promised that "this gospel of the kingdom will be preached in the whole world as a testimony to all nations, and then the end will come." When will the end come? Jesus said after the gospel has been preached to "the whole world" and "all nations." If we're close to that goal, could it also be that we're close to the return of Christ? I believe we are.

That takes us to the other Great Commission finish lines: the Bible in every language and a body—a church—in every place. Even after there are believers in every nation, the church should and will keep working to make sure that they all have access to the Bible in their own language. And the frontier of God's Kingdom will continue to push out through evangelism and church planting among the world's unreached peoples. We'll talk about those two missions in the next two chapters.

CHAPTER 7

The Bible in Every Language

The Bible promises that God's Kingdom will include people from every nation, every place, and every language. Today God's "every language" promise is being fulfilled through the effort to translate the Bible into the heart language of every person on earth. In this chapter, we'll consider why Bible translation is important, how the work is being accomplished, and where we stand in the push to see the Bible in every language.

WHY TRANSLATION?

Christianity, like Judaism before it, is based on the written word. God in his wisdom chose to record his dealings with people in a book—the Bible—that faithful Christians believe to be true, accurate, and reliable. Our faith is anchored in Jesus, but our knowledge of him and what he has done comes through Scripture. It is through the Bible that we learn about God, his love for us, his plan to save us, and how we are called to live.

That's why access to the Bible is foundational to a strong, maturing Christian faith. And it's why, almost from the beginning, God's people have worked to translate God's Word into the languages people speak. Having access to the Bible in the language we know best is critical to discipleship.

THE HISTORY OF TRANSLATION

Bible translation began in the third century BC with the Septuagint, the Greek translation of the Hebrew Old Testament. It's called the Septuagint, meaning "seventy" in Greek, because it was produced by seventy (actually seventy-two) Jewish scholars. It made the Old Testament accessible to the Greek-speaking world, including early Christians. Most of the Old Testament quotations in the New Testament are from the Septuagint.[1]

Having access to God's word in the language we know best is foundational to a strong, maturing Christian faith.

The spread of Christianity across the Roman Empire created the need for the Bible in Latin. Around 400 AD, Jerome produced what became known as the Vulgate Bible, which remained the official Bible of the Catholic Church until the twentieth century.

But Latin was not the heart language of most people, which created a need for so-called vernacular translations. Beginning in the fifth century, translations were produced in the Armenian, Syriac, Coptic, Old Nubian, Ethiopic, and Georgian languages. [2]

In the fourteenth century, John Wycliffe, a scholar and preacher in England, produced the first English translation of the Bible. His translation, completed around 1382, was based on the Latin Vulgate. Though his work was groundbreaking, he faced fierce opposition from church officials who feared that ordinary Christians lacked the spiritual discernment to handle Scripture rightly—but also that giving ordinary believers direct access to God's Word would undermine the church's power. After his death, the church condemned him, exhuming and burning his bones—with as many of his Bibles as they could find.[3]

The invention of the printing press in 1440 exploded access to the Scriptures, opening the door to mass-produced vernacular Bibles. The first of those was Martin Luther's German Bible. Completed in 1534, it helped shape both German Christianity and the German language and became a foundational text for the Protestant Reformation.[4]

Around the same time, William Tyndale translated the New Testament and much of the Old Testament into English. Like Wycliffe before him, Tyndale's efforts were met with fierce opposition from the church and government. He was persecuted, exiled, and ultimately executed in 1536. But his work lived on, forming the foundation for later English translations, including the King James Version.[5]

Similar efforts were underway in France, Spain, Portugal, Russia, and other European countries.[6]

The King James Version (KJV), commissioned by King James I and published in 1611, is perhaps the best-known Bible translation. It was a monumental achievement, involving forty-seven scholars who worked from Hebrew and Greek texts as well as Tyndale's English translation. It was the standard English Bible for centuries—some still consider it the best English translation—and profoundly influenced both faith and language.[7]

Bible translation surged during the nineteenth century's missionary revolution. Robert Morrison completed his Chinese translation in 1823[8] and Adoniram Judson his Burmese translation in 1840.[9] William Carey finished the Bengali Bible in 1809, and also worked on translations for Sanskrit, Oriya, Assamese, Hindi, and Marathi.[10] Other nineteenth-century missionaries similarly prioritized Bible translation.

By 1900, the full Bible was only available in about 100 of the world's 7000+ languages.

Yet by 1900, the full Bible was available only in about 100 of the world's 7,000-plus languages. Another 400 or so had some Scripture: the New Testament or a few books.[11] While those 100 languages reached much of the world's population, hundreds of millions still lacked access to God's word.

But the twentieth century brought a new surge. Cameron Townsend founded the Summer Institute of Linguistics (now SIL Global) in 1934 and Wycliffe Bible Translators in 1942. Together, these organizations have transformed Bible translation.[12] In 1993, Wycliffe launched Seed Company with the goal of accelerating Bible translation by empowering indigenous teams.[13]

THE BIBLE IN LASAMIT

Faheem wept. "I cannot imagine a day when my people will have God's Word in our language." Faheem, a high school physics teacher, was one of only two Christians among the Lasamit, a large unreached people group in an Islamic African country. He had been learning about Church-Centric Bible Translation and how God had used it to bring Scripture to the Haryani people of India.

Faheem said, "My friends and I often talk about the strife and bloodshed in our country. In Islam, you never find teaching about loving and forgiving people. We were even taught in school about killing each other. But Christianity teaches us about love and forgiveness–that you forgive even those who hurt you." He wanted to tell his people they could live in peace.

Like many, Faheem believed he was not qualified to translate God's Word for his people. But as he learned about Church-Centric Bible Translation, he saw a way. He now leads the Lasamit translation team with Greater Reach Alliance. Since 2021, his team has translated the fifty unfoldingWord Open Bible Stories (OBS), including audio recordings, plus books of the Bible into Lasamit.

The impact has been dramatic. Over 150 Lasamit have accepted Christ, and a dozen Lasamit house churches have been planted. Dozens of Lasamit come to Christ each month as they listen to the recording of OBS in their language. And the Lasamit have now composed the first praise songs in their language.

The gospel has come to the Lasamit!

UNDERSTANDING LANGUAGE

There is a joke that gets laughs around the world because its punch-line is so true: "What do you call someone who speaks only one language? American." Because most Americans are monolingual, there is much about language and translation that we don't understand.

Heart Languages and Shared Languages

For one thing, we don't appreciate the difference between a heart language and a shared language. For most of us, they are one and the same: English. But in many places—and especially among minority people groups—people have both a native, or heart, language and a second, shared language.

At home and in their village, they use their heart language: the language they dream in, joke in, and pray in; the one they learned as infants; their native language. But when they communicate with people outside their *ethnos*—in the marketplace, at the government office, at the medical clinic—they use a shared language. This is often the language they learned in school. Sometimes it's a European language; sometimes it's the language of a larger nearby people group. In West Africa, it might be Hausa; in East Africa, Swahili; in India, Hindi; in China, Mandarin.

By 1900, the full Bible was only available in about 100 of the world's 7000+ languages.

For example, my friend Daniel, a Nigerian missionary, speaks four languages: his heart language, Karekare; the trade language, Hausa; English; and Kanuri, which he learned to evangelize them.

And that's not unusual in Nigeria, with its hundreds of people groups and languages.

If we only needed to get the Bible into languages that everyone could understand, we would be nearly done. With the entire Bible in over 700 languages, most people already have access to God's Word in a language they comprehend. But the goal is to get Scripture into the *heart language* best understood by every person on the planet. That is a much bigger task. But imagine for a moment having God's Word only in some language you know and not in the language of your heart, and you will quickly understand why this task is so important.

Oral Languages

Many of the world's languages have no written form. People in these oral language groups do not read or write, and they have no newspapers or books—they communicate only through spoken language.

Traditionally, translators working on oral languages begin by developing an alphabet. They then teach the people to read and write and enlist their help in translating the Bible into their new, written language. As you can imagine, this adds a lot of time and complexity to the translation task. What's more, it takes time for an oral culture to adapt to the written word, including written Scriptures.

Today, ministries like Faith Comes By Hearing and Spoken Worldwide are spearheading oral translation, using audio recordings and mobile apps to deliver God's word to oral language communities. These spoken Scriptures reach hearts more naturally in oral cultures, bringing the message of the Bible alive for them.

The Deaf

Think for a second about how you learned language. At first, no one taught you—you picked it up naturally as you listened to people speak. Before long you were speaking, learning new words and forming them into sentences. Then you were taught about letters, and one day someone showed you three letters and said, "This means 'cat,'" and you were on your way to learning to read and write.

Now imagine that you were born deaf. Because you can't hear, that first step of language acquisition is short-circuited. Likely your parents don't know a sign language, so they can't teach you. Only if you live in a place with a deaf school—and have parents who value your education and can afford it—will you ever learn formal language. Even then, you'll probably struggle with written language. What's worse, in many places your disability is seen as a curse, further isolating you. This is the life experience of many of the 35 million deaf people in the world today.

> The deaf are regarded as distinct people groups, with their own languages and cultures, everywhere in the world.

Because of the fundamental difference in the way the deaf acquire language, they are regarded as distinct people groups, with their own languages and cultures, everywhere in the world. And their languages—often variations of American or European sign languages—are included in Jesus' "every language" mandate. Because sign languages are visual, sign language Bibles are videos, not books. And while Bible translation is always expensive and time-consuming, that is even more true with video Bibles.

Sadly, progress in deaf translation has been slow. The first sign language Bible—American Sign Language—wasn't completed until 2020.[14] But the work is accelerating. Organizations like the International Mission Board (IMB), Wycliffe Bible Translators, and DOOR are now prioritizing deaf translation. Today, there are more than 150 active sign language Bible translation projects underway worldwide, and 75 have published at least some portions of Scripture.[15]

The Evolution of Language

Languages are fluid: Meanings, pronunciation, and grammar evolve over time, and new words are invented or adopted from other languages. In some cases, these changes produce new dialects or even entirely new languages. Languages can disappear as their speakers migrate toward more widely used shared languages. And in today's connected world, these shifts are happening faster than ever.

All this affects Bible translation. Languages that are fading away may no longer require translation. We'll see at the end of the chapter how it impacts the remaining work. Older translations—like the King James Version—can become dated and require revision. For example, consider this verse from the KJV: "For the mystery of iniquity doth already work: only he who now letteth will let, until he be taken out of the way" (2 Thessalonians 2:7). In the seventeenth century, *let* meant to restrain or hold back; today, its meaning is exactly the opposite: to permit or allow. The New King James Version addresses this change, using *restrain* instead of *letteth* in this verse.

WHY IS TRANSLATION DIFFICULT?

Bible translation is complicated. The Bible was originally written in Hebrew, Aramaic, and Greek—languages with their own unique grammar, idioms, and vocabulary. Finding precise equivalents in modern languages for each word, phase, and idea is often challenging. Translators must determine how to convey the meaning of a passage faithfully while making the translation natural and clear.

Translators aim for the Bibles that are accurate, clear, and natural.

For example, consider the problem faced by John G. Paton, a nineteenth-century missionary to the New Hebrides (now Vanuatu), who struggled to find a word in the local language for "faith." One day, he noticed a local man leaning back in a chair. He asked the man to describe what the was doing, and adopted the phrase meaning "to lean one's whole weight upon" to express the concept of faith.

Cultural context adds another layer of complexity. The Bible was written in a unique historical and cultural setting. Metaphors, customs, and social norms familiar to the original audience can be obscure or misleading to new hearers. Translators must find ways to make these cultural elements understandable while preserving the integrity of the text.

For instance, when the first Moravian missionaries went to the Inuit people of Greenland, they had to find a way to express the idea of Jesus as the Lamb of God to people who had never seen sheep. Ultimately, they arrived at this culturally relevant dynamic equivalent: Jesus, the Seal of God.

Theological nuances are also challenging. Various denominations and traditions have different ideas about topics like baptism, gender roles, and the end times. Translators must navigate those differences, cognizant of how their own theological biases might shape their work.

Translators aim to produce Bibles that are accurate, clear, and natural. *Accuracy* describes the faithfulness or fidelity of the translation to the original. It ensures that the translation reflects the original intended message as precisely as possible, without adding or omitting meaning. *Clarity*—also referred to as *intelligibility*—ensures that the text is easily understood by the audience. This involves, among other things, translating idioms, metaphors, and cultural references in ways that make sense in the target language. *Naturalness* means that the translation uses comfortable, familiar phrases, vocabulary, and rhythms. This prevents the translation from sounding foreign or artificial.

HOW IT'S DONE

Traditionally, translation has been the domain of academics. The early translators, like Luther and Tyndale, were educated theologians who knew Greek, Hebrew, and Latin. Of course, they were also fluent in their own language and so were perfectly positioned to bring God's Word to the vernacular.

This academic approach continued into the twentieth century. Typically, a Western couple would be trained—at the MA or PhD level—in Greek and Hebrew, linguistics, and translation. They would then go and live among the language group, learning the target language. If necessary, they would produce an alphabet

MADAGASCAR

The Word of God first came to Madagascar in 1835, when it was translated into Malagasy, the island's primary language. But there are twenty-three other language groups in the country representing approximately 30 million people. Over the years, some translation has been done in these groups, but much remained to be done.

But a few years ago, God put a burden for those languages on the Zoar Hope Church Ambohipo in Antananarivo, Madagascar's capital city. God has uniquely positioned this church across the street from a university that draws students from language groups all over the country. The church pulled together 300 volunteers—many of them students—to draft Bibles in four languages in four years—an amazing achievement!

One of those was the language of the 200,000 Sihanaka people of northeastern Madagascar. Thanks to this translation, the Sihanaka now experience God's Word in a new, deeply personal way. Razafinjaka, a translator for the Sihanaka Bible, explained the impact: "When people get the Word in a language that is clear to them, that is evangelism, and they will believe in Jesus Christ."

What started with one church has now grown. Ten other churches have joined Zoar Hope Church to form a consortium for Bible translation. Together, they are launching translation projects to bring the blessing of God's Word to eight more people groups in Madagascar. Working together in humility and unity, these churches are accomplishing far more than any one of them could achieve alone. Through them, God is fulfilling His "every language" promise for Madagascar.

that allowed the language to be written. They would then teach the people to read and write, enlisting their help in understanding the nuances of the target language.

Often translation would start with a story book—Jonah or Ruth—or with the Gospel of Luke, and proceed from there to other New and Old Testament books. Typically, the process took several decades— essentially the lifetimes of the translators.

Many courageous and faithful men and women used the traditional model to translate the Bible into hundreds of languages.

This model relies on translation consultants to oversee and review the work of the translation teams. These consultants are highly educated linguists and theologians who review drafts, verify theological accuracy, check for consistency, and identify any potential misunderstandings or cultural misinterpretations. They help ensure that the translation aligns with both the source text and the linguistic and cultural nuances of the target language.

Many courageous and faithful men and women used this model to translate the Bible into hundreds of languages. But it has weaknesses. For one thing, it is fragile, based on the slender thread of the small translation team. It is not unusual for teams to be forced to abandon work on a language due to illness, exhaustion, political instability, or persecution. For another, it requires significant academic ability, which only a few possess, and high-level training, which is expensive and time-consuming. Furthermore, because Western translators are not native speakers of the target languages, their translations sometimes score low on clarity and naturalness. And because the work is done primarily by the translators, sometimes the resulting Bible is regarded as foreign by its audience, even though it is in their language. Finally, completing a translation using this approach can take decades.

Seed Company

To overcome these difficulties, in 1993 Bernie May and John Bender-Samuel of Wycliffe Bible Translators founded Seed Company. Their goal was to empower local, native language translators and churches, speeding the work and producing translations that were more natural and authentic.

The impact has been remarkable. Since 1993, Seed Company has completed thousands of translation projects: many New Testaments, some Old Testaments, and even some full Bibles. They've engaged with nearly half of all languages that have Scripture and as of June 2025 they are working in 1,405 languages. Other translation ministries have adopted Seed Company concepts into their own processes.

Technology

Technology has revolutionized Bible translation. Tools like Paratext, Adapt It, and Translation Studio automate tasks and improve accuracy, consistency, and accessibility. Render enables translation in oral languages, capturing spoken drafts for communities without a written language. Programs like these streamline translation, reducing both cost and time.

Artificial Intelligence (AI) may soon help even more. AI can help speed translation by suggesting words and phrases, checking for consistency, and even sensing cultural nuances. But AI must learn the target language before it can help with translation, and doing that requires a body of text in the target language—ideally related passages of Scripture, but at least books, magazines, or newspapers— for training. That's no problem for major languages, but many smaller languages—and all oral languages— don't have that. Nevertheless, AI will undoubtedly help accelerate and improve translation.

AI will undoubtedly help accelerate and improve translation.

Church-Centric Translation

Church-Centric Bible Translation (CCBT) is a powerful, grass-roots approach to Bible translation that places the local church at the center of the process. Unlike traditional models that depend on outside translators and academic experts, CCBT equips local believers to translate Scripture into their own language. This speeds up translation and boosts clarity and naturalness. The process also disciples the local church and strengthens its ownership of the final product.

Instead of the original Greek and Hebrew texts, CCBT translation efforts usually begin with a "gateway language" Bible—a shared-language translation that serves as the bridge to the target language. For example, in India the process for a new translation might begin with the Hindi Bible. Many models of CCBT use new economy principles like crowd-sourcing and iterative development to replace the experts in the traditional model.

Small teams of translators work side by side to wrestle through choices of words and idioms. They then share their drafts with other teams to check their work. When those checks are complete, the entire group reads the second draft and makes further corrections. Software tools are used for theological and error checking. And even when the translation is ready for use, it is not considered finished but is subject to regular review and iterative improvement. And all the while, the translators are being discipled through their daily interaction with the Word of God.

Church-Centric Bible Translation equips local believers to translate Scripture into their own language.

Generally in CCBT the translators are believers—sometimes new believers—but there are instances where nonbelievers are invited to participate in the work in a new language. I know of one people group in Sudan where most of the original translation team were Muslims. When they figured out that the book they had gathered to translate was the Bible, some quit, but others persisted. It shouldn't surprise us that many of the translators became Jesus followers after being so deeply exposed to God's Word.

Many CCBT efforts begin with Bible stories instead of books. For example, unfoldingWord, a leading ministry in the CCBT space, has a target set of fifty stories with which they begin their translation efforts.[16]

Not only does CCBT lower the cost of translation—it also produces translations faster than traditional methods, often with higher clarity and naturalness. And while some worry about the accuracy of CCBT translations, the iterative approach of CCBT assures that quality will improve over time. CCBT also results in deeply equipped local leaders who can go on to create additional new resources for worship and discipleship for their churches.

COLLABORATION

Historically, the world's Bible translation ministries—Wycliffe, Seed Company, Pioneer Bible Translators, Biblica, and others— operated independently. These ministries were collegial, but there was little collaboration among them, resulting in duplication and inefficiency.

But between 2010 and 2013 a group of influential donors came together to encourage collaboration. They helped leaders of Bible translation ministries see that cooperation could accelerate the pace of translation dramatically and make possible what then seemed impossible: translating the Bible into every language in this generation.

Their initial goal was to create an accessible Digital Bible Library housing all the translations from every ministry. The donors requested that the CEOs of the top translation ministries meet monthly to work on the DBL and to build relationships. Fifteen years later, the result is a unified translation movement with significant cross-ministry coordination and a set of shared goals for completing Bible translation.

When God's people come together openhandedly, they are answering Jesus' John 17 prayers.

NIGERIA

Bible translators have historically considered Nigeria to be one of the "Big Five" places—the five countries and regions with the most languages still needing translation. As recently as 2022, approximately 250 languages in Nigeria still were waiting for Bible translation.

But in early 2023, a meeting of five ministries—including the Nigeria Bible Translation Trust and Faith Comes By Hearing—resulted in the launch of the Aminci Cluster project. *Aminci* is a Hausa word meaning "trustworthy" or "reliable." This four-year project is committed to bringing God's Word to forty-nine people groups in their heart languages.

Fast forward to November 2023, when another meeting took place to address remaining language needs—this time including nine ministries. This gathering produced plans for translating another 105 languages, impacting over seven million people.

"What's happening is a move of God," said Jackson Vusaka, a Bible translation leader in Africa. "Previously, Bible translation has been the work of Western Bible agencies. But of late we've seen God touching the hearts of church leaders. They are saying, 'God has called us to do Bible translation. We don't know how that's going to look or be, but we want to do it!'"

And that's exactly what is happening. As churches are stepping up, the list of Nigerian languages waiting for Bible translation is shrinking, from 250 in 2022 down to a few dozen today. That's unprecedented, not only in Nigeria but in the history of Bible translation. God is on the move, accomplishing his "every language" promise in Nigeria.

In 2014 and 2015 this alliance moved from operational collaboration to collaborative fundraising. It's hard to overstate how bold a move this was: If operational collaboration is hard, raising funds collaboratively is almost unheard of. Ministries are protective of the relationships they have developed with their major donors and are reluctant to risk exposing them to the work of their peers. Nevertheless, these leaders stepped out in faith to see what God would do. They came together to form the illumi*Nations* Alliance and host an annual collaborative fundraising event.

The results have been spectacular. In their most recent annual gathering in April 2025, about $50 million was raised to support translation. That brings the total to almost $480 million that has been contributed at the eleven illumi*Nations* gatherings—a very significant part of the roughly $1 billion the Alliance estimates will be required to finish the "every language" mandate.[17]

It's worth asking why Illumi*Nations* has been so wildly successful. I think there are three reasons. First, they provide a great experience that has built a tight community of donors who embrace the "every language" goal. More importantly, by coming together, the illumi*Nations* member ministries can present a much bigger and bolder vision than any of them could offer alone. That bigger vision inspires donors and leads to bigger donations. Third—but perhaps most importantly—when God's people come together openhandedly, they are answering Jesus' John 17 prayers that we "may be one" as He and the Father are one. The Father loves His Son and is inclined to bless anything that responds to the Son's prayer for our unity—which illumi*Nations* certainly does.

WHERE DO WE STAND?

The experts say that the word's eight billion people speak more than 7,300 languages. About one billion are native speakers of the largest language, Mandarin. The top twenty-five languages (Mandarin, English, Spanish, Hindi, and so on) have about five billion native speakers. From there the numbers get smaller and smaller, and the world's smallest 1,000 languages have only a few thousand or even just a few hundred speakers each.[18]

By the grace of God, it is possible that in less than ten years Scripture will be available in every one of the world's unique languages.

As I write this in 2025, the full Bible is available in 756 languages spoken by almost six billion people. The New Testament has been translated into another 1,726 languages, covering another 800 million people. Another 1,274 languages spoken by about a half billion people have at least some portions of the Scripture—stories, chapters, or books.

That means that there are 3,756 languages with some or all of the Bible and that seven billion people have access to God's Word in their heart language. But that still leaves more than 3,000 languages and about one billion people with little or no heart-language Scripture.[19]

illumiNations has analyzed the remaining languages and has determined that many of them will not require translation—in most cases because the language is heading toward extinction. In other cases, no translation is needed because the people are so fluent in a shared language that it has become like a second heart language. These decisions have reduced the target for translation from 7,300 languages to around 6,000.

And there is an amazing plan for finishing the work. illumi-*Nations* has set the following targets—its "All-Access Goals"—to be accomplished by the end of 2033:

- Ninety-five percent of the world's population (7.6 billion people) will have access to the full Bible in their heart language.
- Of the world's population, 99.9 percent (7.96 billion people) will have access to the New Testament in their heart language.
- Of the world's population, 100 percent will have access to at least some portion of Scripture in their heart language.
- There will be two viable Bible translations in the world's 100 most strategic languages[20].

What's most exciting is how the pace of work is accelerating. According to Illumi*Nations*, out of the 6,000 remaining languages, 2,845 have met their All-Access target, including 250 that met the goal in the year ending March 2025—a record pace. Another 2,542 are in progress—translation work has begun in these languages, but the goal for them has not yet been achieved. Only 518 remain that have not yet been started.

And the rate of new starts is rapidly increasing. The goal for new translation starts for the year ending March 2025 was 150 languages, but work actually began in 356.[21] It's really happening!

CONCLUSION

When John saw people from every language worshipping around the throne of God, he had no idea how many languages there were—only that all of them were present. And for much of history, just counting all the world's languages—much less translating the Bible into all of them—would have been impossible. But today, thanks to the hard work of generations of God's people, advances in technologies and methodologies of translation, collaboration, and the generosity of many donors, the global church has the "every language" goal in sight. By the grace of God, it is possible that within the next ten years Scripture will be available in every one of the world's unique languages. What a great day that will be for God's Kingdom and his people.

CHAPTER 8

A Body in Every Place

Many in the church these days are eagerly anticipating the second coming of Christ. But for billions of people in the unreached world, Jesus has yet to come the first time. They've never heard his name—or know him only as a prophet of Islam—and have no idea what he has done for them. They are in utter spiritual darkness.

As we learned in chapter 6, the gospel is very close to reaching every people group. But in many of those groups, there is only a handful of believers. Those groups are engaged with the gospel, but only barely. Consider, for example, the Malay people. There are almost 14 million Malays in Malaysia, and only about 0.1 percent of them—maybe 14,000 people—are Christians.[1] The typical Malay will never encounter another Malay who knows Jesus. And the Malay are just one of hundreds of similar frontier people groups.

Jesus didn't just command us to make a few converts in every people group—he commanded us to take the gospel to every place on the planet—to "the ends of the earth"—so that "the earth will be filled with the knowledge of the glory of the Lord as the waters cover the sea."

How can we fulfill Jesus' commands to preach the good news and make disciples everywhere? The answer is through church-planting and disciple-making movements. And the vision is that by the end of 2033, these movements will result in a church—a Body of Christ—being planted in every place people live on the planet.

WHY CHURCHES?

If Jesus had simply told us to preach the gospel in every place, the task would be nearly done. Thanks to technology—radio, television, the Internet, and so on—the earth is being saturated with gospel proclamation, and many are coming to faith.

But Jesus did not just tell us to preach and make converts—he commanded us to make disciples, teaching them "to obey everything that I have commanded you" (Matthew 28:20). Making disciples requires more than just preaching and evangelizing—it requires community.

The Christian life is not meant to be lived in isolation. It is in community that we are sanctified as we learn to practice the New Testament's "one another" commands. It is in community that we use our spiritual gifts, those special abilities God has given every believer "for the common good" (1 Corinthians 12:7). In community we find accountability, encouragement, and love that help us stand firm when things get tough. Finally, there is special connection to Jesus when groups of his people assemble. As he promised,

"For where two or three gather in my name, there am I with them" (Matthew 18:20).

Making disciples requires more than just preaching and evangelizing—it requires community.

Jesus' people have always obeyed his command to make disciples by planting churches. Beginning with the apostles, wherever God's people have gone with the gospel, they have planted churches. That's still true today as the gospel advances into the world's unreached people groups and places.

WHAT IS A CHURCH?

When you hear the word *church*, you probably think of your church. It has a building where you gather. It has one or more pastors, typically employed full-time and probably seminary educated. It has hundreds or thousands of members. It's the primary place where you hear God's word taught, where you worship, where you give, where you serve, and where you fellowship with other believers. You may have been married in a similar place, and when you die it is where your life will be remembered.

The churches that are being planted today in unreached places are much simpler. They typically don't have dedicated buildings but meet in homes. Their pastors are usually not paid but support themselves through farming or a trade. Most have not been to seminary but have been trained in God's word and church leadership in a less formal way. These simple churches are generally much smaller than we are used to—sometimes as small as just eight or ten people.

What do these house churches do? Like your church, they gather regularly to worship, study the Scriptures, and pray. From time to time, they celebrate the Lord's Supper and baptize new believers. They serve and love one another.

George Patterson, a missionary and church planter, identified seven foundational commands of Christ to guide new believers in their discipleship journey: repent and believe, be baptized, pray, make disciples, love, observe the Lord's Supper, and give.[2] Some practitioners add "worship and develop leaders" to this list. Healthy house churches do all these things.

One thing these house churches emphasize that we often neglect in the West is obedience. They hold one another accountable for putting the things they learn into practice. Paul Eshleman liked to tell about a time he asked a house church pastor in India to tell him what he did in his church. The man answered, "We listen to God's Word, we talk about what it means, and then we do what it says." Paul would say he laughed and told the man, "Well, at home we do two of those three things."

By stressing practical obedience—"doing what it says"—house churches can quickly build healthy spiritual habits in those who are coming to faith. And that includes, importantly, the practice of sharing one's faith continually.

It is important to recognize that the Bible also uses the word *church* to describe the universal church—the collection of all Jesus followers in every *ethne* everywhere in the world throughout history. It was this universal church that Jesus established when he said in Matthew 16:18, "I will build my church, and the gates of Hades will not overcome it." As God's people work to plant local churches everywhere in the world, we are building this amazing, multi-ethnic, God-glorifying global church and bringing Jesus' promises to fulfillment.

> By stressing practical obedience—"doing what it says"—house churches can quickly build healthy spiritual habits in those who are coming to faith.

MOVEMENT

There is one more thing that these simple house churches are expected to do: multiply. The members of these churches are encouraged—as soon as they believe, and sometimes even before—to share Christ with their friends, relatives, and associates and to plant new churches as those people come to faith. Multiplication is in the DNA of these house churches—they are designed to be churches that plant churches that plant churches. And sometimes, when the Spirit moves, these multiplying churches can become what is known as a *movement*.

Today much church planting around the world is focused on igniting movements. Only God can launch movements—like the wind, the Holy Spirit blows where he pleases (John 3:8)—but God's people can create the conditions that may lead to a movement through fervent prayer and faithful practice of certain basic, reproducible processes.

Multiplication is in the DNA of house churches–they are designed to be churches that plant churches that plant churches.

That isn't a new idea, but it had been lost until Roland Allen reintroduced it in his book *The Spontaneous Expansion of the Church*, published in 1962.[3] George Patterson further developed the idea in his 1976 pamphlet "Obedience Oriented Education," which showed how lay pastors could be trained to multiply churches through simple obedience-based discipleship.[4]

Jesus told his disciples, "The harvest is plentiful but the workers are few. Ask the Lord of the harvest, therefore, to send out workers into his harvest field" (Matthew 9:37–38). Movements activate the millions of Christians around the world into an army of workers for the harvest field.

There are two flavors of movement: disciple-making movements (DMM) and church-planting movements (CPM). They differ slightly in their approach—DMM emphasizes gradual discovery leading to salvation and discipleship, while CPM prioritizes intentional gospel presentation and church formation followed by discipleship—but both aim to see rapid multiplication of disciples in previously unreached places.

PASTOR G

When Pastor G became a Christian, he committed himself to sharing the gospel with his countrymen. He worked hard, and after twelve years he had planted fourteen churches.

But he wanted more. He heard about church-planting movements and reached out to e3 Partners for help. They sent trainers from the United States to teach Pastor G and his team about simple church. Over the course of two weeks, as those trainers taught and modeled movement, forty-two churches were planted!

Pastor G was convinced—forty-two churches in two weeks was far better than fourteen churches in 12 years! He embraced DMM and began to use the methodology to plant churches that planted churches that planted still more churches.

Today he leads a movement of the gospel that reports 500,000 churches and 4 million followers of Jesus across a wide swath of his South Asian country. And leaders from his movement have begun traveling to other countries to launch new movements.

Both DMM and CPM have proven to be enormously effective, and they are not mutually exclusive—many ministries combine elements of both. For example, New Covenant Missions uses a DMM approach when working among Muslim people groups in Africa and CPM while working with animist groups.

Disciple-Making Movements (DMM)

Movements begin with prayer. A trained believer—a well-discipled disciple-maker—will ask God to connect him to spiritually open people, perhaps in his workplace, his village or neighborhood, or someplace nearby. As God answers that prayer, the believer begins building relationships. Often this involves praying for his new friends, in the name of Jesus, seeking healing, deliverance, or some other blessing.

At the right moment, he asks if they'd like to know more about Jesus. If they say yes, he invites them to invite their friends, and together they begin a Discovery Bible Study (DBS). They meet to hear God's word and talk about what it teaches them about God and people and what they should do to obey it. Rather than overtly sharing the gospel, DMM opens the door for God's word to change the hearts of the participants. Instead of being told or taught, they discover the truth about God and his good news for themselves as they study and discuss God's Word.

DMM emphasizes gradual discovery of God's Word leading to salvation and discipleship.

Discovery Bible Studies use Bible stories to guide seekers and new believers through the Bible's redemptive narrative. The study might begin with Creation, the Fall, Noah, Abraham, and so on. Or it might begin with New Testament tales like the Prodigal Son or Zacchaeus and build from there into an exploration of the person and life of Christ. The goal is to immerse the participants in Scripture, sparking personal discovery that transforms hearts and minds.

DMM pursues rapid multiplication by encouraging the participants to share what they've learned with their friends and relatives and to invite them to join a DBS. This begins growth before anyone has been challenged to accept Christ.

Many have learned DMM through a training called Zúme, from the Greek word for yeast. Zúme equips ordinary believers to launch movements that spread rapidly, like yeast through dough (Matthew 13:33). Created by veteran missionary Curtis Sergeant, Zúme teaches essential disciple-making practices like prayer walking, identifying persons of peace, and DBS. Zúme also introduces a simple model for house church, Three Thirds, which emphasizes discipleship, accountability, and mission.[5]

A DBS is not a church, but over time it can become one. Instead of just reading and discussing God's Word, the participants begin to worship and pray for one other. As the group matures, it begins practicing the sacraments, such as baptism and the Lord's Supper.

Some criticize DMM for being indirect, but the DMM approach has achieved amazing results, especially in resistant places. In his book *Miraculous Movements*, Jerry Trousdale explores the extraordinary growth of disciple-making movements among Muslims. The book highlights stories of transformation as individuals and families embrace the gospel through DBS.[6]

Among the top DMM practitioners are New Generations, Final Command Ministries, and BigLife. Each of these ministries is using DMM techniques to make disciples and plant churches in resistant places around the world. You can learn more about them at their websites listed at the back of this book.

Church-Planting Movements (CPM)

Like Disciple-Making Movements, Church-Planting Movements (CPM) aim for rapidly expanding movements of churches and disciples. But CPM moves more quickly toward the formation of churches, which disciple new believers over time.

CPM prioritizes sharing the gospel quickly with as many people as possible and forming churches quickly.

As with DMM, CPM begins with and is sustained by prayer. Often the first step involves church planters prayer walking in an unreached place. They pray for God to remove opposition and to connect them with a person of peace. This phase may last days or, in spiritually resistant areas, weeks.

Once, in a meeting in Nepal, I asked a team of experienced church planters if they ever got the person of peace wrong. They looked at me as if I had lost my mind and replied, "We ask the Holy Spirit to show us the right person, and he does." Their answer is an important reminder that all this work is undertaken in the powerful name and with the unseen support of Jesus Christ.

Once the church planters feel led, they enter the village and engage with the person of peace God has prepared. At the right time, they share the gospel, using tools like Three Circles, the Bridge Illustration, or a Creation to Christ story. If the person professes faith, the church planter will encourage him to share what he has received with family and friends, inviting them to learn more about Jesus. That person's home often becomes the first church's meeting place.

CPM methodologies vary, but one popular model is Four Fields, developed by IMB missionary Nathan Shank. Using a simple farming metaphor—planting, cultivating, harvesting—Four Fields guides believers through the stages of starting and multiplying churches.[7]

THE FOUR FIELDS OF JESUS' STRATEGY

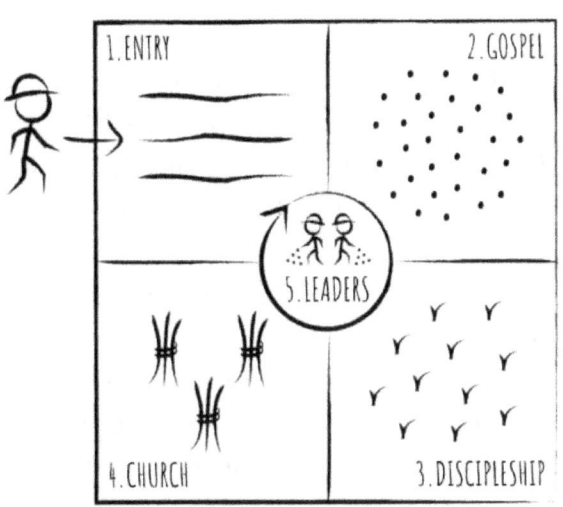

Another effective model is Training for Trainers (T4T). Designed by Steve Smith and Ying Kai, T4T starts with basic training that includes how to share your testimony, present the gospel, and begin a simple house church using the Three Thirds model. From there, each person is expected to train others using the same process, creating a multiplying chain of discipleship.[8]

Ministries using these and similar approaches include East-West Ministries, e3 Partners, The Timothy Initiative, Cru/Global Church Movements, Team Expansion, and Operation Mobilization. Each of these has its own variations on the model, but all are seeing remarkable fruit as they train and mobilize indigenous believers to plant churches in the world's unreached places.[9]

Movement

Movement is achieved when the DMM or CPM effort in a place begins to experience "multiplication of disciples making disciples and leaders developing leaders, resulting in multiple streams with four or more generations of indigenous churches planting more churches."[10] Once a movement is ignited, thousands of small house churches can be planted in a relatively short time—and the world's largest movements, in India and China, now extend to over a million churches.

Once a movement is ignited, thousands of small house churches can be planted in a relatively short time.

The role of Westerners varies from ministry to ministry—some use Western leaders to provide training and oversight, while others rely on national leaders—but the day-to-day work is invariably in the hands of ordinary, local believers.

It may sound chaotic, but there is order to the process. Each church in a movement is connected to the church from which it was birthed. That church-to-church link—which extends from the smallest, newest churches back to the movement's founders—becomes the structure for overseeing the new churches, handling issues that arise, and measuring the growth of the movement.

In many movements, each church planter collects information on the churches he has planted and those downstream from them, sometimes on paper or sometimes using software like GenMapper or iShare. These maps show the relationships between the various churches in the network and report on the health of each church. This simple tool allows leaders to assess how each church is maturing and to locate patterns of strength or weakness in the network that require attention.

Each church planter in the chain also regularly evaluates those under his care to decide who God is equipping to take on greater responsibility in the movement. Those selected receive additional training and may be sent to new locations to begin a new family of churches. Likewise, those who are ineffective, carnal, or abusive are also identified and removed from the field for additional training or discipline.

What About Doctrine?

Wait a minute, you might think. *Isn't movement an invitation for heresy and abuse? Don't these church planters need to be thoroughly trained and supervised?* That's a real concern—although it's worth remembering that Western churches, with the world's most highly trained clergy, are also susceptible to doctrinal error and poor leadership.

Movements mitigate the risk of heresy and abuse through accountability, regular Scripture engagement, and a culture of obedience. Training is decentralized and new leaders are equipped

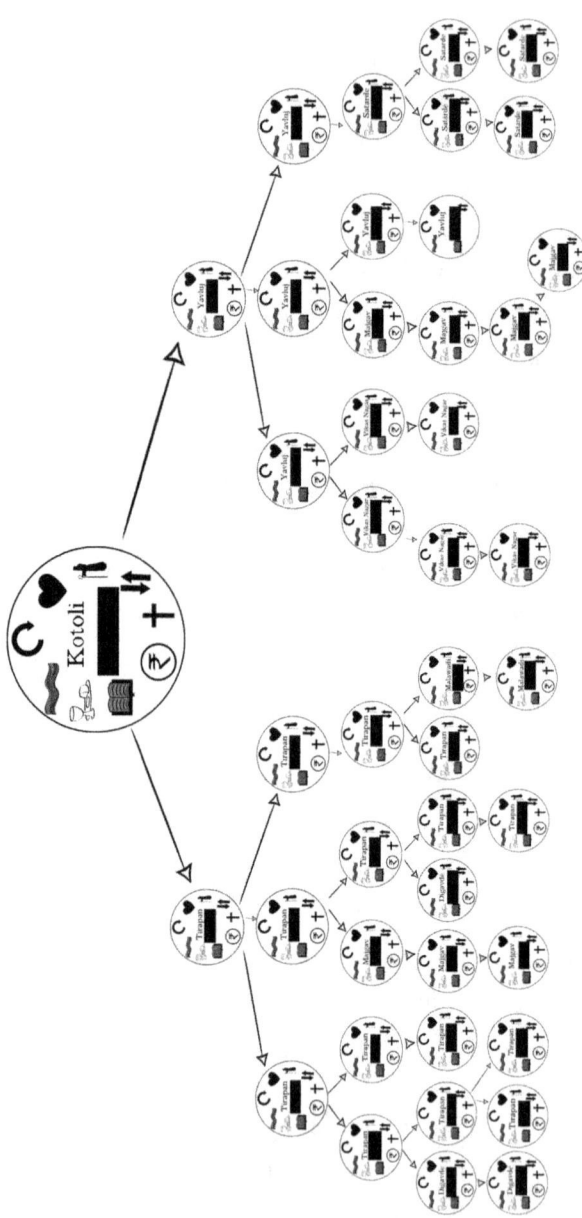

through real-time learning and immediate application. They're coached by more experienced believers and learn as they do the work day by day. The model isn't perfect, but it reflects the New Testament pattern and fuels exponential growth.

Some years ago, veteran missionary Bill Smith was asked to audit a very large movement started by Ying Kai in a restricted Asian country. He tracked the movement through twenty-seven generations and found that the church planters

> Movements mitigate the risk of heresy and abuse through accountability, regular Scripture engagement, and a culture of obedience.

were implementing the training exactly as it had been taught to the first generation of leaders. In other words, throughout twenty-seven generations of reproduction, there had been zero drift in doctrine or practice.[11]

Impact

Movements have profoundly impacted global evangelism in the last forty years. They've led to the rapid increase of disciples and churches, especially in places previously resistant to the gospel.

According to the 24:14 Coalition, in early 2025 there were over 1,966 movements worldwide, encompassing more than 115 million believers in approximately 9 million churches. Another 3,600 pre-movements are being pioneered, with over 1,700 of those seeing second- and third-generation churches. These movements have been particularly effective among unreached people groups, with

A STORY OF MOVEMENT

This is a story of how the Good News has spread in one South Asian movement.

Ganesh shared the gospel with a young man named Vikas. He accepted Christ and was discipled.

One day Vikas took a group of believers to a village to pray over sick people. While there he shared the gospel with Bajrang, a young man who sold moonshine from his house. When Bajrang accepted Christ, his transformed life became a great testimony in the whole village.

Bajrang later met a young man called Kiran, who mocked Christians. When Bajrang shared the gospel with him, the Holy Spirit convicted him, and Kiran accepted Christ.

As Kiran was being discipled by Bajrang, he went to another village and shared the gospel with a young girl named Kavita, who also accepted Christ. She was the only person in the village who believed, but she began to read the Bible, and Kiran discipled her. Now there are seven churches there.

CPMs and DMMs present across the Muslim, Hindu, and Buddhist cultures.[12]

Another church-planting network, the Global Alliance for Church Multiplication (GACx) reports that its 112 member organizations have planted 2,915,496 churches since its founding in 2011[13].

Movements are happening around the world, but India leads the way. One movement, founded by Indian church planter Victor

> Kavita went to a remote village to share the gospel, and Sandeep came to Christ. Now Sandeep has started several churches.
>
> Sandeep shared the gospel with Raju Gaikwad, who was struggling with depression because his wife left him. God began to work in his life as he was discipled by Sandeep.
>
> Raju shared the gospel with an illiterate woman named Harnabaij, who sells brooms house to house. She accepted Christ, and now wherever she goes she presents the gospel.
>
> Harnabaij started a church in her home, which Suvarna began to attend. The church prayed for her and God healed her from heart disease.
>
> Suvarna shared the gospel with Jyothi, a young lady who was always quarrelling with her husband. God transformed her life, and she is witnessing to many.
>
> That's ten generations of believers in a place where historically there have been none, all the result of the simple faithful obedience of ordinary believers.

John, is planting churches among the Bhojpuri people in Bihar State. Bihar, which thirty years ago may have had 10,000 Christians, today has more than 10 million.[14]

Indian movement leaders are beginning to transplant those "hot coals" to other Asian and Middle Eastern countries with the hope of kindling movements there as well. One Middle Eastern pastor shared a dream with an Indian movement leader. A camel was pregnant but unable to give birth. Suddenly, a water buffalo appeared and rammed into the camel, and the camel delivered its calf. The pastor told the Indian leader, "We are the camel, and you are the buffalo. Please come help us birth a movement of the gospel here."

Challenges

Movements are creating remarkable results that would have been unimaginable a few years ago. They vividly illustrate the urgency with which God is working today to see the Great Commission completed. But there is still much left to do. Even after planting millions of new churches, millions more are needed, and significant challenges remain.

One challenge is the dearth of funding going to world's unreached places. Perhaps 40 percent of the world's population—between three and four billion people—live in the unreached world. But only a tiny fraction of all Christian giving worldwide goes toward work among the unreached: $1.32 billion out of $1.3 trillion, or about one dollar out of every thousand.[15]

And out of a global missionary force estimated at 253,000 people, only about 24,000, or 9 percent, are thought to be working among the unreached. In other words, most missionaries work in places where the gospel has already been proclaimed.[16]

Another challenge is rapid population growth in the world's unreached places. Today, sub-Saharan Africa has an estimated population of 1.24 billion people, but it is expected to grow to 1.4 billion by 2030 and perhaps 2.1 billion by 2050.[17] Similar growth is expected in other unreached places. Even if millions come to faith each year, the number of unreached will continue to grow.

An even greater challenge is that no one knows for certain exactly how many places there are that need to be reached, nor precisely where they are. Dividing the world's population—roughly eight billion people—by 1,000—roughly the size of a typical village—yields eight million places. But that's just a guess.

And how many of these places have churches? Individual ministries and movements know where they are working, but they typically don't share that information with others who are planting churches in the same regions. This means that several ministries may target the same places while other places get no attention at all.

Out of a global missionary force estimated at 253,000, only about 24,000 are thought to be working among the unreached.

What's more, even the data we have is sketchy. There are undoubtedly errors and some duplication in the reported results. Sadly, there is probably even some duplicity in these numbers. When financial support depends on reported results, the temptation to overreport can be strong.

COLLABORATION

Several excellent networks and collaborations of church-planting ministries are working to overcome these challenges. The 24:14 Network is a global coalition of church planters working to see movements underway everywhere by the end of 2025. This coalition is particularly effective at identifying indigenous church-planting efforts and is working to provide funding for those ministries, which are often invisible to Western donors.

GACX is likewise committed to accelerating church planting worldwide. Their goal is a church for every 1,000 people everywhere on the planet.

The Coalition of the Willing

You might think that it would be easy to get church-planting ministries to share their data. After all, if everyone shares, everyone benefits. But ministries typically are reluctant to share data, in part due to security concerns. And the resistance can be passionate—an evening gathering on data sharing at the 2019 Finishing the Task Conference came as close to blows as any Christian meeting I've ever attended.

The Coalition of the Willing is a collaboration of ministries willingly sharing data about the locations of their churches.

But after that meeting, the leaders of two leading church-planting ministries—Scott Cheatham of e3 Partners and Jared Nelms of The Timothy Initiative—agreed that they would share their data with one another *and* with any other ministry that would join them. That was the beginning of the Coalition of the Willing (COTW)—a collaboration of ministries willingly sharing data about the locations of their churches. Five years later, twenty-five ministries have joined COTW, including East-West Ministries, the Southern Baptist IMB, and Cru/Global Church Movements.

EDWING

Edwing lives in Maicao, Colombia. He grew up in a Christian home and always wanted to be a pastor–a dream he realized when he was twenty years old. Edwing loved God and desired to see the church grow and for others to come to know God. His denomination sent him to plant several churches in different parts of Colombia. But there was one thing missing that he longed to see: a multiplication movement in the church.

Edwing began to search for help online. To his surprise, he discovered that there are movements of the gospel starting in different parts of the world through something called Disciple Making Movements (DMM). God led him to the Big-Life website, and BigLife's interim director for Latin America, Moy Soriano, traveled to Maicao, where for two days he trained Edwing and thirty others on what it means to make disciples and practice simple church.

Since that training in January 2024, new believers have been added, baptisms have been held, and ten new house churches have been planted in Maicao and among the Wayuu people in the surrounding the rural areas. Edwing is now planning to take this same vision to other areas of Colombia.

The collaboration is producing results. COTW has invested in a software tool, iShare, that facilitates data sharing and visualization. iShare maps the world down to eight million polygons—each representing one "village"—and allows church planters to share what they know about each one. Should it be red (no believers or churches), yellow (believers but no churches), or green (believers and churches)? iShare protects this sensitive data from prying eyes but gives each participating ministry access to the maps, which they can use to plan their work. As ministries plant churches, they update iShare so that it presents an up-to-date picture.

iSHARE MAP

No Christians, No Churches

Christians, No Churches

Christians and Churches

COTW has selected twenty-one countries for the first comprehensive surveys. One country, Nepal, has already been surveyed.

Togo in West Africa and Sri Lanka are up next. These surveys are collaborative efforts, involving several ministries. Once they are complete, the next step will be to plant churches in every unchurched place in each country. As those countries move toward completion, others will be slotted for surveys, until the task is done.

ACHIEVE

While in theory movements eventually result in churches in every place, in practice they do not. A movement is likely to produce a lumpy result, with many churches in some places but none in others. To address this, new models have emerged that add every-village intentionality to movements.

This idea was pioneered by DAWN Ministries, founded by Dr. Jim Montgomery in 1985. The ministry's Disciple a Whole Nation strategy mobilized denominations and mission agencies to plan and implement large-scale church-planting efforts. DAWN played an important role in catalyzing church-planting movements in Latin America, Africa, and Asia during the late twentieth century, and its vision was adopted by other organizations and networks, including GACx.

The latest expression of saturation church planting is ACHIEVE, an acronym for A CHurch In Every Village Everywhere.

The latest expression of saturation church planting is ACHIEVE, an acronym for A CHurch In Every Village Everywhere. Ministries are undertaking church-planting projects that seek to plant a church in every village within some defined geography: one of more blocks or districts (like counties in the United States) or provinces (like states). They begin with surveys, then use movement strategies—with an added layer of every-place intentionality—to make sure that no gaps are left when the work is finished.

For example, one project led by New Covenant Missions in the African country of Ethiopia is working to plant a church in every unchurched village in two *woredas* (counties). Similar projects are underway in India, Thailand, Sri Lanka, Nepal, and other countries.

Don't let the word village in the ACHIEVE acronym trip you up—it's just a convenient way to say "everywhere people live." In rural settings, that's literally villages, but in cities, "village" might mean a ward or precinct, a suburb, or even a high-rise.

The ACHIEVE vision is being nurtured by a subset of the COTW called the ACHIEVE Alliance. Their prayer is that ACHIEVE will become for church planting what Illumi*Nations* has become for Bible translation: an alliance of ministries multiplying their impact through collaborative fundraising.

WHAT REMAINS?

As I said earlier, no one knows how many unchurched places there are. COTW is working to pin down that number, but for now all we have is an educated guess: at least three to five million new churches will be needed to achieve ACHIEVE. That sounds like an enormous number, but keep in mind that the world's current movements already may be planting close to a million new churches every year. And while most of these new churches need to be planted in hard places, we're already seeing an explosion of new churches in hard places through movements.

MOVEMENT IN THE DESERT

In an arid West African country, a Team Expansion missionary family trained a courageous believer named Hahlev to be a multiplying disciple. Hahlev begin sharing his faith in villages across the region. In one village, the chief believed Hahlev's message, accepted Jesus, and was baptized. Soon, many in the village believed along with him. Over the next few months, Hahlev returned again and again, teaching, training, and helping them build a well. The village finally had drinking water and living water.

One night, a terrible fire struck the village, destroying nearly all the huts. Even so, the people decided they weren't going to let this catastrophe destroy their joy. As they were cleaning up, a representative arrived from a distant village desiring to hear about Jesus. The people stopped their work and prepared a welcoming meal for their guest. He listened as they explained the gospel and went away changed.

Word continued to spread. Today, more than 3,500 villagers in that region have been baptized. Another 2,500 are listening actively to the gospel. Each week 234 simple churches are meeting. There are now believers from four tribes, all of whom were Muslims and previously hostile to outside influences.

Hudson Taylor famously said, "Every great project of God goes through three stages: First, it's considered impossible. Second, it's difficult. Third, it's done."[18] By God's grace, the global church is moving from the impossible to the merely difficult stage of the "every place" effort. And by his grace, it will soon be done.

What will it cost? Estimates vary, but the ACHIEVE Alliance ministries have set the benchmark at $500 per church. That may seem ridiculously low, but remember the dynamics of movement—churches that rapidly plant churches that plant churches—and that this work is happening in places where dollars go further than in the United States.

> By God's grace, the global church is moving from the impossible to the merely difficult stage of the "every place" effort.

Taking that estimate and the midpoint number of churches needed—four million—yields a total cost of around $2 billion. Again, that may seem enormous, but remember that the global church is already giving $1.3 trillion every year. Increasing the share of that going to unreached places to $1.6 billion a year—an additional 0.02 percent of total giving—would provide the needed funds.

How long will it take? The ACHIEVE Alliance is asking God to accomplish the vision by the end of 2033. That's the same finish line illumiNations has prayerfully set for the "Bible in every language" goal. Even more significantly, it is the 2,000-year anniversary of the Great Commission itself. We've been working on this task for 2,000 years—isn't that long enough? By God's grace, isn't it time we finished?

CONCLUSION

Just before Jesus went to the cross, he prayed, "I pray also for those who will believe in me through [the apostles'] message, that all of them may be one, Father, just as you are in me and I am in you. May they also be in us so that the world may believe that you have sent me" (John 17:20–21).

As the global church comes together around the vision of ACHIEVE, God is answering this prayer for unity and dramatically increasing the number of people in the world who believe. By God's grace, over the next few years millions of new churches will be planted around the world—"to the ends of the earth"—and "the earth will be filled with the knowledge of the glory of the Lord as the waters cover the sea." By your grace, Lord Jesus, make it so!

CHAPTER 9

The Great Coming

Jesus told his disciples to go to the ends of the earth and preach the good news, so going is how the gospel should spread. Many throughout history—from the apostle Paul to William Carey to today's missionaries—have been obedient to this model, accounting for most of the gospel progress over the centuries. But when God's people do not go as quickly or as far as he desires, he has other ways to keep his "every nation, every language, every place" promises. In this chapter we'll explore those other methods—involuntary going, involuntary coming, and voluntary coming—and consider how he is using them in our day to accelerate the sprint to the finish. [1]

INVOLUNTARY GOING

Voluntary going can be very hard. And for that reason, only a handful of people in every generation willingly obey the command to go. But God will not allow our desire for comfort and safety to thwart his plans, and so from time to time, when his people have refused to go voluntarily, he has required them to go involuntarily.

Involuntary going is when God's people are forced—against their wills—to leave their reached places and go to unreached places. One biblical example of involuntary going is the scattering of the Jerusalem church, documented in Acts 8. Jesus had commanded them to go, but they wanted to stay in the city and enjoy the amazing blessings of that first church.

> When God's people do not "go" as quickly or as far as He desires, He has other ways to keep His "every nation, every language, every place" promises.

So Jesus sent persecution that forced them to leave Jerusalem for other places: "On that day a great persecution broke out against the church in Jerusalem, and all except the apostles were scattered throughout Judea and Samaria" (Acts 8:1). As a result, the gospel began to spread around the Roman world.

This example yields a memorable aphorism about involuntary going: If the church doesn't obey Acts 1:8, it will experience Acts 8:1.

Another example is the prisoners taken by the Vikings in the ninth and tenth centuries. Because the church had been slow to go to the Norse people—and because God had a purpose for them in the further spread of the gospel—God arranged for some of his people to go as prisoners to Scandinavia. They didn't want to go, but when they were forced to go, they took the good news with them and evangelized their captors.

As I said, voluntary going can be very hard. But *in*voluntary going is almost always harder, often involving the permanent loss

THE GOSPEL COMES TO THE FULGAN

The Fulgan people live in a mountainous region of one of Africa's poorest and most violent countries. Virtually all Fulgan are Sunni Muslims; there are few if any Christians among them. In fact, until very recently no one had ever bothered to take the good news of Jesus Christ to them.

But recently, a team of two Christian women from a nearby people group began ministering among some displaced Fulgan people living in a refugee camp. And the Lord has begun to work in miraculous ways.

One Fulgan woman was demonically possessed. She had not eaten or spoken for four days. When her family tried to read to her from the Quran, she ripped it apart. She left her hut and began sleeping in the camp graveyard. But when the two Christian women found her, they prayed for her, and she was instantly delivered. Thanking God, she gave her life to Christ!

Another Fulgan woman was seriously ill. The team found her at her home surrounded by concerned family members. After explaining that they would pray for her in the name of Jesus, they sent the family out of the hut. As they prayed, she was healed instantly and stood up. They called her surprised husband and showed him what had happened. And they told her to go tell her friends and family what Jesus had done for her.

The gospel has come to the Fulgan!

of freedom and family and even the loss of life. Think of those Jewish exiles and the early Christians. God does not want his people to suffer unnecessarily, but he is serious about keeping his promises and so is willing to orchestrate circumstances that force his people to go.

INVOLUNTARY COMING

The gospel can also be spread by coming, both involuntary and voluntary. If God's people won't go from the reached world to the unreached, God can bring the unreached world to them—whether it wants to come or not.

A biblical example of involuntary coming is the peoples that the Assyrians relocated from various parts of their empire to Samaria: "The king of Assyria brought people from Babylon, Kuthah, Avva, Hamath and Sepharvaim and settled them in the towns of Samaria to replace the Israelites. They took over Samaria and lived in its towns" (2 Kings 17:24). These people would become known as the Samaritans, and hundreds of years later, one of them, a woman, would meet Jesus by a well near Sychar. Her ancestors didn't want to come to Samaria, but they did, and for that reason she—and many others in Samaria—met Jesus.

Perhaps the greatest example of involuntary coming in history is the African slave trade. From around 1500 to about 1850, millions of Africans were stolen away from their homelands and families and brought to the West as slaves. They came against their wills and at a horrendous personal cost.

The African slave trade was a great evil. But God can use great evil to accomplish his purposes, and that is what he did in this case.

There are already millions of Africans in heaven who encountered Jesus while enduring slavery, and even more of their descendants who will be saved because of living in the reached world. They didn't choose to come here, but God used that great wickedness for their eternal good.

Today we are seeing involuntary coming as refugees from wars, famine, and persecution flee their homes for safer places. Some of these refugees make it to the West; others make it only to a refugee camp outside the borders of their country. We'll consider shortly how God is working through these involuntary comings to build his kingdom.

VOLUNTARY COMING

The final way God spreads the faith is voluntary coming. Voluntary coming occurs when the unreached world comes voluntarily to the reached world.

We saw a couple of examples of voluntary coming in the Old Testament in chapter 2: Naaman, who came to Israel voluntarily seeking healing, and the Queen of Sheba, who came voluntarily to investigate Solomon. Maybe the best historical example of voluntary coming is those same Vikings we just talked about. They came as pagan invaders to Christian Europe, and the result was very bad for the Christians. But as we've said, the result of their voluntary coming was that the people of Scandinavia were Christianized within two generations and became aggressive spreaders of the good news themselves.

Often, voluntary coming means invasion, where a pagan people will conquer a Christian people. The result is often politically and

FROM ANGRY TO KIND

Omar and Samira and their children Imed and Hamdi are an Afghan family that has lived in the Vahdat camp in Tajikistan for three years. One day, a Team Expansion missionary named Abdul met Omar while distributing food. After some time, he offered Omar a Bible, which Omar began to read.

One night, Omar had a dream of a man in a flowing white robe who gave him a box containing a radiant book. When Omar woke up, he texted Abdul and told him about the dream. Abdul encouraged Omar to continue reading, and he began to study the Scriptures with him.

Omar was amazed by the things he was learning and began practicing and sharing everything he was gleaning. He stopped beating his wife and children. His face changed from angry to kind and loving.

As Samira witnessed the changes in her husband, she decided that she wanted to follow Jesus as well. It wasn't long until Abdul baptized Omar and then Omar baptized his wife!

Today, Omar and Samira are growing in the Lord and leading a group in their humble apartment. God has used Omar to plant multiple WhatsApp house churches in Afghanistan, and he has a vision to see churches in every part of the Vahdat area and throughout all provinces in Afghanistan.

economically disastrous for those who are invaded, but throughout history voluntary comings have resulted in the salvation of many of the invaders.

THE GREAT COMING

We are living today through the greatest coming in the history of the world. Millions are making their way from the Global East and South to Europe and America. Some are coming voluntarily for economic opportunity; others, involuntarily, to escape war or persecution.

Estimates are that between 2000 and 2024 the number of international immigrants grew from 150 million to over 304 million[2]—and that's up from just 84 million in 1970.[3] In 2015 alone, the Syrian refugee crisis brought more than a million people to the safety of Greece, Germany, Sweden, and other Western European nations.[4] In the United States, approximately 30 million individuals obtained lawful permanent resident status between 2000 and 2024.[5] Another 10 to 20 million have come illegally, mostly from Central American countries like Honduras, Guatemala, and Mexico but some from nearly every country on earth.[6]

We are living today through the greatest coming in the history of the world.

Politically, this great coming is a white-hot issue, and for good reason: Its political and economic implications could be dire. The issue of unchecked immigration and what to do about it divides voters and parties throughout the democratic West. It even divides believers.

But there is another, spiritual layer to this great coming. It has eternal consequences that far exceed its secular impacts. I'm not saying that it's wrong to oppose unchecked immigration or that the secular effects are unimportant, but only that there is also an enormous kingdom impact from this great coming.

Think of what God is doing: He's bringing millions of lost people from some of the world's hardest places into the most reached countries in the world. He's told us to go, but in his grace—both to them and to us—he's bringing the nations to us. Consequently, we need only go across town—and not around the world—to tell them the good news. Many—perhaps millions—of these migrants will come to know Jesus through their coming to the West. None of them came for that reason, and most would tell you it could never happen to them, but God, whose purposes always prevail (Proverbs 19:21), will use their coming for their eternal good.

Working Among the Immigrants

Many great ministries have seized the eternal opportunity presented by the great coming. Global Gates, founded in 2012, focuses on making disciples among unreached people groups in cities like New York, Houston, Detroit, and Toronto. Their missionaries live in immigrant communities, sharing the gospel, planting churches, and training new believers to reach others—both locally and in their home countries. It's the same disciple-making process used around the world, but it's happening right here in North America.

THE MAN WITH THE LAMB ON HIS SHOULDERS

Matt is a Global Gates missionary serving refugees in Pennsylvania. His friendship with an Iraqi refugee led to an introduction to her brother Jadeed, who also had fled Iraq.

As they talked, Jadeed told Matt about dreams he'd had nearly two years earlier. In the first, he entered a house with many strangers. Suddenly, a majestic person entered the room. Jadeed felt he knew this man but could not remember his name. The man smiled at each person in turn, then looked at Jadeed—his eyes full of love—and said, "Come unto me." Jadeed woke up, troubled by this dream and the identity of this unknown man.

About a week later, Jadeed had a another dream. The same man appeared, carrying a lamb on his shoulders, and said, "Come unto me, you who are lost." The next morning, Jadeed searched on the Internet, "Who is the man with a lamb on his shoulders?" The answer came back: "Jesus."

Jadeed told Matt he wanted to know more about Jesus. Matt told him that the words from his dreams were from the Bible and encouraged Jadeed to read it for himself.

Over the next month, Jadeed read the entire New Testament. When he talked with Matt again, he said he was convinced that Jesus was God and that he wanted to follow him. Since then, Jadeed has led seventeen others to faith in Christ. Because they are scattered in several countries as refugees, they study the Bible together using WhatsApp.

Global Frontier Missions (GFM), based in Atlanta, began its "home hubs" in Atlanta and Houston in 2010 with two goals: to evangelize unreached immigrant populations in the US and to train new missionaries for overseas service. In Atlanta's Clarkston suburb—home to refugees from 65 countries and 90 unreached people groups—GFM missionaries prayer walk, build relationships, and lead Discovery Bible Studies. As people come to faith, they form house churches or connect with existing ethnic congregations.

International Project targets diaspora unreached people groups (UPGs) in global cities like Dallas and Rome. In Rome, their Agape Center offers language classes and cultural activities to build relationships and share the gospel. Their Equip Missionary Training Program, a ten-month immersion in New York City, trains participants in church planting among unreached communities.

In my hometown, a young couple with Team Expansion is serving Afghan refugees—teaching English, helping with job applications, and providing transportation and housing. As they build trust, they share the good news. Their goal is to get a heart language Bible to every family, and they're now distributing solar-powered audio Bibles in Pashto and Dari.

Many local churches are doing the same in their own cities—helping immigrants navigate government systems, teaching practical skills like sewing and welding, tutoring kids after school, and looking for every chance to share the gospel. Some have even launched house churches or satellite campuses for new immigrant believers.

Europe

There is also great opportunity in Europe, where many excellent ministries are reaching immigrant populations. All Nations International and Greater Europe Mission are partnering to plant churches among Muslim immigrants in Germany. Working together, they've planted thirty-one churches since 2016. Now they're endeavoring to plant a hundred immigrant churches in thirteen German cities over the next three years. These efforts are not only reaching Arabs, Afghans, Kurds, and others in Germany—they're also sparking new churches in the immigrants' home countries. So far, sixteen churches have been planted abroad as new believers share Jesus with friends and family back home.

Refugee Oasis partners with local churches in France and Spain to provide essential services and share the love of Jesus. They train volunteers to teach weekly language classes for immigrants, using prepared lesson plans. At the end of each six-week session, students are invited to a Jesus Night—an evening of food, games, and Scripture reading in both their new and native languages. Those who express spiritual interest are invited to join a Discovery Bible Study. Through this simple model, thousands are encountering the gospel.

One leader from the No Place Left network reports on their work among refugees in Europe. Their frontline team includes many former refugees—Iranians, Arabs, Afghans, and others—who have come to Christ. They minister in Greek refugee camps, introducing new arrivals to Jesus, discipling them, and even planting churches. But most of these refugees soon move on to Western Europe, where established believers help plant new churches

SEEKING KNOWLEDGE, FINDING FAITH

Zisong grew up an atheist in China. He knew no one who followed Jesus and considered religion to be useless superstition.

When he was nineteen, his mother developed cancer. For the first time he began thinking about religion and exploring Taoism. Some of it made sense, but the picture was blurry. Still, he was convinced that there was something beyond the material.

He later came to UC Irvine as a graduate student. He learned about Bridges (CRU's international campus group) and joined their gatherings—not because of spiritual interest, but for the free food. They invited him to Bible study, but he declined—he wasn't interested in American religion.

At the same time, though, he was increasingly overwhelmed by the pressure to excel. When he shared those feelings with his Bridges friends, he was struck by how kind and caring they were. He realized what they had wasn't just

in Germany, France, and beyond. No Place Left now networks with 400 Afghani believers, 300 Kurds, and a growing group of Pakistanis—all in Germany.

The most exciting result of the work is how the gospel travels back to the refugees' home countries. As they come to faith in Christ, they tell their friends and family at home the good news. Some even return as near-culture missionaries to their own people. No Place Left is seeing great fruit from the work of these missionaries—who first voluntarily came to Europe but then religion but a power inside them that enabled them to love him so well.

Then one night, a pastor connected the gospel to Chinese culture, explaining that it is the specific revelation of the Tao. He was amazed to learn that the Chinese Bible used Tao to translate the word *logos*: "The Tao was God." He began reading the Bible and was struck by its practical wisdom. He recognized that he was the proverbial lost sheep—that he was lost and needed a loving Shepherd. At that moment, he was crushed. Everything else became insignificant. He needed nothing else but Christ.

Bridges leaders discipled Zisong and taught him how to share the gospel. God also convicted him about the need to tell his countrymen about Jesus. When he returned to China, it was as a missionary, and today Zisong helps train pastors in rural China.

voluntarily returned home—in some of the world's most restrictive countries.

Refugee Camps

The Great Coming isn't all voluntary—many come as refugees to escape war, persecution, and natural disaster in their homelands. A few find their way to the United States or Europe, but many are stuck in teeming refugee camps around the world—places like Kutupalong and Nayapara in Bangladesh, where nearly a million

Rohingya refugees have fled persecution in Burma, or Dagahaley, Hagadera, and Ifo in Kenya, where hundreds of thousands of Somali refugees survive.

Try to imagine living in such a place: thousands of people packed into makeshift shelters, with no electricity or clean water, cut off from friends, family, and community, with no clear idea about the future. It's a bleak existence, but it creates huge opportunities for the gospel. When everything familiar is stripped away, people can be more open to the gospel.

So even in these terrible places, the gospel is moving. John Becker of AIM and 3P Ministries reports that local partners are seeing the beginnings of a movement of the gospel in the Gorom refugee camp in South Sudan, which houses 20,000 refugees from Sudan, Ethiopia, and the DRC. Believers serve the refugees and build relationships through trauma healing, food security, agriculture, and small business development services, then share the gospel with them. Many are coming to Christ, and many churches are being planted.

In His great mercy, God has brought many through hardship from a place where they might never have heard of him into His kingdom.

Team Expansion is working among the Afghan refugees who have fled to the Vahdat region of Tajikistan. More than 17,000 people live there in dilapidated Soviet-era apartment buildings, with more arriving every week. They receive no assistance from the Tajik government. Conditions are poor, electricity is sparsely available, and most live hand to mouth.

In 2023 Team Expansion's Tajik national partners identified a handful of Christian families among the refugees. They invested in relationships with these families, taught them how to share their faith, and equipped them with supplies for their neighbors—things like blankets, basic food items, and hygiene products. While delivering these items, the believers build relationships and seek families of peace. As they've shared the gospel, the Spirit has moved, and there are now over a hundred newly baptized believers and forty-eight home groups meeting among the Afghans.

Over two million refugees from the horrible civil war in Myanmar have fled to Thailand over the last few decades. mPower Approach serves these communities with free dental and eye care and tells them about Christ. Many are coming to faith, and dozens of churches have been planted. Despite the civil war, some choose to return to Myanmar with the gospel; others join the small but thriving churches that have been formed there.

Education

Education is another powerful driver of the Great Coming. Every year many of the world's best and brightest make their way to the United States for higher education.

This trend has increased significantly over time. According to Open Doors, there were about 1.1 million international students studying at American colleges and universities in 2024, up from about 500,000 in 2000 and about 150,000 in 1970. Many come from gospel-difficult places: India, China, Vietnam, and others.[7]

Many campus ministries—including Intervarsity, Navigators, and Chi Alpha—are working to reach these students. Cru's Bridges

REZA

Reza was born in Pakistan. From a young age he was instructed in the Quran, sharia, and jihad. He became a Hafiz (someone who has committed the entire Quran to memory) and won gold medals in Quranic recitation.

In 2005, he was sent to Athens as a Muslim missionary, concealed among the flood of Muslim refugees entering Europe. His mission was jihad. He hated Christians and believed dying for Islam was the only sure path to heaven.

He began working for a Christian couple in their store. He despised them as *hadath*–unclean–but was moved by their kindness and honesty. They even encouraged him in his prayers! This perplexed him and stirred a spiritual search.

Then one night, Reza dreamed of a man in white who said, "Go to church." His employers took him, where he had a vision: The cross transformed into a throne, and on it sat the man from

International serves international students on dozens of campuses across the US and Canada, helping them with language and organizing small-group activities including Bible studies. Friends of Internationals is another ministry focused on this opportunity. They partner with local churches and volunteers to connect international students with Christian families, who provide support, including transportation and meals, opening opportunities to share the faith.

God is bringing these future leaders from their unreached homes and planting them in our backyards. Like all young people his dream. He said, "Reza, I've been waiting for you for a long time." Reza asked, "How can I come in my sinfulness?" The man said, "Give me all your sin; I will wash it away."

Transformed, Reza resigned his ministry and returned to Pakistan, where he faced severe persecution. To escape, he walked back to Europe—this time as a real refugee. He worked in a restaurant until one night the Holy Spirit said, "I did not bring you here to cut vegetables." Soon after, he met David, an American missionary, who started training him in disciple making and church planting.

Reza began working among the 1.5 million Muslim refugees in Germany. He has since started forty-seven refugee churches in Germany, and his disciples have taken the gospel back to their homes and to other European countries. He is a wanted man, but God has protected him and made him a fisher of men.

far from home, they're lonely and confused and need love and care. And as we'll see in chapter 13, they present a great opportunity for you to become a Great Commission worker.

URBANIZATION

Related to the Great Coming is the powerful trend toward urbanization around the world. Urbanization has been happening for decades in the United States, but it is also occurring in every country on Earth: Every day young people leave their farms and villages and move to the city in search of opportunity. This is the driver behind the explosive growth of many developing world cities— places like Lagos and Cairo whose populations have swelled to tens of millions.

Today, more than half of the world's population lives in urban areas, a sharp increase from just 30 percent in 1950. According to the United Nations, this trend is expected to continue. An estimated two-thirds of the global population is projected to live in cities by 2050.[8] The cities of sub-Saharan Africa (excluding South Africa) are doubling in population every eighteen years, and some are expected to exceed 80 million by 2100.[9]

Like the Great Coming, this trend toward urbanization serves to accelerate the Great Commission. Because there is some Christian presence in nearly every big city in the world, it is more likely for a person to encounter Jesus in a big city than in a village. That may happen through an encounter with a believer, through a radio or television broadcast, or through access to the Internet—all things that may not be present back home.

It is difficult to quantify the Great Commission impact of urbanization. No one knows precisely how many people live in these megalopolises, much less what they do each day or who they are meeting. But we know through Global Media Outreach and other similar ministries that many people are encountering Jesus in these places via the Internet.

One ministry focused on church planting in cities around the world is Redeemer City to City. Founded by Tim Keller, founding pastor of Redeemer Presbyterian Church in New York, Redeemer City to City trains and equips leaders to cultivate gospel movements in global cities through church planting. Their vision is to see the gospel of Jesus Christ transform lives and impact cities. To date they have trained over 150,000 leaders and have helped plant over 2,000 churches in 150 cities worldwide, including Johannesburg, Kuala Lumpur, and Mumbai.

Two Four Eight is a global ministry focused on launching and multiplying DMMs in cities. Founded in South Africa in 2001, it equips teams in urban centers with training, coaching, and tools tailored to complex, multicultural environments. Their strategy emphasizes affinity-based networks—groups formed around shared cultures, languages, or interests—to ensure that discipleship efforts are both relational and reproducible. Today, they are working toward a vision of 1,000 transformational urban movements.

> Even as we are straining toward the goal, God is moving it closer to us.

CONCLUSION

Many of God's people are striving with all their might to reach the Great Commission finish lines. But even as we are straining toward the goal, God is moving it closer to us. We are going to the world, but the world is also coming to us, through immigration—voluntary and involuntary—education, and urbanization. I believe God is accelerating the work through these means because he knows that time is short and the harvest is plentiful. By his grace, the Great Coming will add millions to the multitude that will soon gather around the throne of God.

CHAPTER 10

Media and Technology

Have you ever thought about how much technology has advanced in your lifetime? We live in an age of astounding innovation, and we take for granted all manner of wonders that our great-grandparents would have regarded as science fiction: the Internet, smart phones, joint replacements, GPS, and many more.

This isn't accidental. Daniel 12:4 predicts that in the last days, "knowledge will increase" (NLT). We're certainly living that reality today. But I also believe that God intended some of these innovations to help accelerate the Great Commission. This chapter will explore how technology and media are being used to proclaim the gospel to the world.

FILM AND VIDEO

Film—and later video—were enormously impactful innovations of the twentieth century, revolutionizing the worlds of entertainment and communication. So it shouldn't be surprising that visual media has also had an immense impact on the Great Commission.

The JESUS Film

The JESUS Film is the most important tool for global evangelism since the printing press. Released in 1979 by Campus Crusade for Christ (now Cru), this cinematic portrayal of the gospel of Luke has brought the story of Christ to more people, in more languages, in more places, than any other resource in history.

Translation

From its inception, Cru intended *The JESUS Film* to be accessible to people of many languages. Working from translations by Wycliffe, Seed Company, and others, Cru's teams of trained linguists and native speakers have translated the film into over 2,200 languages, making it the most translated film of all time.[1]

The Jesus Film is the most important tool for global evangelism since the printing press.

Modern technology has taken this work to new levels of speed and efficiency. *The JESUS Film* Project uses cutting-edge audio recording systems and software tools that synchronize dialogue with the on-screen action. Portable recording studios, which fit in suitcases, enable teams to travel to remote places to work directly with native speakers on new translations. What once took years can now be done in weeks.

Strategy

At first, Campus Crusade endeavored to have *The JESUS Film* shown in theaters and on television in countries around the world.

One notable showing, in the early 1990s, was on national television in the former Soviet Union. Millions reportedly responded to the message of Christ. The film has also been broadcast in India in Hindi, Tamil, Telugu, and Bengali.

But billions of people don't have access to theaters or television. To address that need, Campus Crusade recruited film teams to show the film in remote places around the world. Equipped with portable projectors, generators, and screens, they would show the film under open skies at night in remote villages and on urban streets.

Often, entire communities would gather to watch the film, many seeing a movie for the first time in their lives. I have been privileged to witness several of these showings over the years, and they were always amazing. Seeing hundreds of people sitting under the stars, captivated by the story of Jesus, gasping as he raised a little girl to life, weeping as he was crucified, and finally cheering as he was resurrected, is deeply moving.

The impact of this strategy was massive, with tens of millions worldwide indicating a desire to follow Jesus. But it had weaknesses. Because the mobile film teams were poorly equipped to disciple those who professed faith, often the fruit from showings would wither away over time. And though Cru deployed thousands of film teams, they still were able to reach only a small fraction of the unreached world.

In response, in the 1990s *The JESUS Film* Project pivoted. Instead of supporting their own film teams, they decided to empower church-planting and disciple-making ministries who would use the film in their evangelistic efforts. Since these ministries were committed to the places where they would show the film,

DISAPPEARING INTO THE STORY

Morgan Jackson of Faith Comes by Hearing was traveling in Ghana with his friend Reverend Theo Asare. To show Morgan the impact of the audio Bible, Reverend Asare stopped in the small Konkomba village they were driving through. They walked into the community and got permission from the chief to play the audio Bible. Soon, everyone had gathered under the shade of one of the few trees in the village. Reverend Asare explained to the people what they were doing and began playing the Konkomba audio Bible for them. As they listened, Morgan watched the people disappear into the story.

They played the Bible for about thirty minutes. Reverend Asare then asked who wanted to accept Jesus as their Lord and Savior. About half of the people raised their hands. Morgan was amazed! They prayed for the new converts, appointed a village leader to oversee further community listening, and gave them an audio Bible.

As they prepared to leave, the Konkomba leaders shared how missionaries had been in this area for some twenty years but had seen only a handful of conversions. Now, after listening for thirty minutes in their own language—hearing Jesus' genealogy, his story, his teachings—they had accepted him as their Savior. A people who had worshiped idols for centuries gave them up because they had heard God speak to them in their heart language. They now knew that Jesus was the real God!

they could better follow up with those who responded. The result has been to increase dramatically the film's reach and impact.

Technology

Over the years, the generators and projectors of the early days have been replaced with smaller, more efficient equipment, such as solar-powered projectors and digital devices. Much of this innovation has come from a great partner ministry, Renew World Outreach. Where once a small truck or a couple of motorcycles were required to transport the equipment for a showing, today the entire package—power source, projector, speakers, and screen—fits in a backpack.

Even more exciting, though, are the innovations enabled by smartphones, tablets, and streaming platforms. The film in every translation is now instantly available everywhere through *The JESUS Film* website and app. Many times, I've enjoyed asking a taxi driver in some US city about his native language, then asking if he'd like to see a film in it. They are nearly always astounded when the sounds of their mother tongue emanate from my phone.

What's more, the film is now being distributed in restricted countries secretly, person to person, on USB drives and SD cards and through encrypted apps.

Another exciting innovation is a new app, PG Studio, created by Mars Hill Productions. This app makes it possible for anyone anywhere to translate media—including *The JESUS Film*—using only a mobile phone. Even with the extensive resources of the JESUS Film Project, translating the film into all the remaining languages will take decades. But PG Studio will give missionaries and indigenous church leaders the ability to translate and dub the film into their own languages without help from outsiders. And PG Studio isn't only for translating *The JESUS Film*—it will also facilitate the translation of the rest of the Bible and other Bible-based media.

Impact

The impact of *The JESUS Film* has been astounding. The film has been shown in 230 countries and territories—that's basically all of them—and has been viewed 8 billion times. More importantly, over 600 million people—more than the populations of North America and Western Europe combined—have made decisions for Christ after watching the film. No other tool or method of evangelism even comes close—and as ministries continue to use the film, the numbers will continue to grow.[2]

Bible Media Group

Bible Media Group is another ministry using visual media to reach the world. Their LUMO Project Films—*lumo* is the Esperanto word for "light"—are visualizations of Scripture. They are used by churches, missions agencies, and individuals to help bring the Scriptures to life, promoting deeper engagement with the Bible.

LUMO's four gospel films are high-quality visual presentations of the Gospels of Matthew, Mark, Luke, and John, using the word-by-word Scriptures as their scripts. *The Covenant* is a ninety-minute film covering the first five books of the Old Testament. Told through the eyes of Ezra, it tells the stories of Adam and Eve, Noah, Abraham, and Moses word by word. And the newest LUMO film covers all twenty-eight chapters of the Acts of the Apostles.

Bible Media Group has a vision for seeing these films available in all the world's languages, and through their partnership with Faith Comes by Hearing, that vision is being accomplished. So far, the four gospel films have been translated a total of 1,574 times. *The Covenant* is already available in 100 languages.[3]

THE GOOD NEWS FOR ORAL PEOPLES

As we learned in chapter 6, many of the world's unreached people groups only use oral communication. For many years, missionaries would address these oral language groups by developing written language and teaching people to read as they translated God's word—in effect drawing them into Western models of learning and communication. But in recent years many have begun to engage oral cultures as they are, with tools that share the good news in audible form.

Faith Comes by Hearing

The leader in this space is Faith Comes by Hearing (FCBH). Founded in 1972, FCBH started with a simple but audacious mission: making the Bible accessible to everyone. Over the decades, they've become the global leader in audio Bibles. Their calling is to record the Bible in as many languages as possible and distribute those Bibles in formats that people can use.

FCBH collaborates with heart-language speakers to capture faithful audio recordings of God's Word. They also produce dramatized audio Bible stories, with multiple voices, music, and sound effects, that are effective tools for Discovery Bible Studies in oral communities.

Thanks to Fath Comes By Hearing, over 2,342 languages and dialects, covering billions of people, now have audio scriptures.

Thanks to FCBH, over 2,342 languages and dialects, covering billions of people, now have audio Scriptures. Through partnerships with ministries and churches around the world, these resources are available in over 200 countries and territories, and over 1.2 billion people now have access to God's Word in audio form.[4]

These audio Scriptures are accessible through FCBH's own audio player called the Proclaimer, which FCBH makes available to church-planting and disciple-making ministries globally. It runs on solar power, a hand crank, or electricity and features a loudspeaker system capable of reaching groups of up to 300 people. Over the years, tens of thousands of Proclaimers have been distributed.

FCBH recordings are also available on solar-powered audio devices produced by MegaVoice. Where the Proclaimer is designed for large group settings, MegaVoice devices are better suited for personal use or small group discipleship.

FCBH has also embraced mobile technology. Their Bible.is app provides access to Scripture in text and audio form on Apple and Android mobile devices. This same content can be accessed via web browsers.

A BEARDED STRANGER

The Sauria Paharia people live in the remote hills of South Asia. Most of them follow the traditional religion of their region. Most Sauria Paharia villages are remote and rarely receive visitors, so sightings of anyone from outside are unusual.

One day the people in one village saw a bearded man walking on the paths above their village. No one knew who he was, and before they could find him, he was gone.

Not long after, two outsiders came to the village with *The JESUS Film* in the Paharia language. The people in the village had never seen a movie in their own language, so they were very interested. When the villagers saw Jesus for the first time on screen, they were shocked–he looked just like the bearded man they had seen earlier.

They continued watching the film and learned about Jesus–his life, death, resurrection, and forgiveness. That day hundreds of Sauria Paharia decided to follow Jesus, and later thousands followed. Because of his great love for them, God made it so that the villagers saw Jesus walking among them as a stranger. Now they know him and call him a friend.

Other Audio Bible Providers

FCBH isn't the only ministry working to provide audio Scriptures to oral peoples. Audio Scripture Ministries helped pioneer this work, producing and distributing audio recordings of Scripture in hundreds of languages. ASI created Talking Bibles International to deliver rugged, solar-powered audio Bible readers.

Spoken Worldwide takes a different but complementary approach. Rather than starting with written text, they begin with oral Bible stories developed in collaboration with local believers. These stories are crafted to be biblically faithful, culturally relevant, and easy to memorize and retell. Once finalized, the stories are recorded in the local language—often with dramatization, music, and sound effects—making them accessible to entirely oral communities. Their approach—called Oral Bible Translation—has proven especially effective in cultures where storytelling is central.

INTERNET EVANGELISM

The ubiquity of cell phones has transformed how people connect, communicate, and access information worldwide. Today, there are about 8.31 billion cell phone subscriptions globally—more than the earth's population! More than seven billion of them are smartphones.[5] The rapid expansion of mobile networks and affordable devices has made tools like Bible apps, audio Scriptures, and online discipleship platforms more accessible than ever and created unprecedented opportunities to share the gospel.

Global Media Outreach

Global Media Outreach (GMO) is a pioneer in the effort to reach people online. Founded in 2004 by Walt Wilson, a former Apple executive, GMO shares the gospel with hundreds of thousands of people, in nearly every country, every day, by connecting seekers with the message of Jesus online.

GMO uses targeted online advertisements, social media campaigns, and search engine optimization to attract spiritual seekers to their sites. Once online, they receive clear explanations, in a language they understand, about who Jesus is and why he came. Each presentation includes an invitation, and those who say yes are connected with trained online missionaries for encouragement and discipleship. New believers are also given digital resources like Bible reading plans, prayer guides, and discipleship materials and are encouraged to connect with local Christian communities.

GMO operates in thirteen languages—including Chinese, Hindi, and Arabic—making their material accessible to three-quarters of the world's population. And GMO strives to explain gospel concepts in ways that are relevant to people in cultures around the world.

Global Media Outreach shares the gospel with hundreds of thousands of people, in nearly every country, every day.

Take a moment to surf to the GMO homepage (https://global mediaoutreach.com), where you'll find a world map and see dozens of pins popping up every minute— each one indicating another gospel interaction. Notice where the pins appear—in Egypt, Iran, Turkey, India, and other challenging places.

A man in Iran, searching online for answers about Christianity, stumbled onto a GMO website. After connecting with a volunteer responder, he gave his life to Christ. Today, he is sharing his new-found faith with his family. A woman in India, searching for peace, clicked on an ad that led her to GMO. She prayed to accept Christ and, through follow-up with a volunteer, began reading the Bible and attending a house church.

The results are incredible. GMO reports over 2.8 billion gospel presentations and nearly 317 million indicated decisions for Christ thus far. In 2022 alone, GMO reported over 260 million gospel presentations and 28 million decisions. And thanks to the economics of the Internet, the cost is extremely low—about $0.10 per gospel presentation.[6]

GMO is not the only ministry to be leveraging the power of the internet for the Great Commission. Others, like Frontiers and Pioneers, use targeted digital campaigns to engage specific language groups and cultural contexts.

The Gospel on the Sly: LightStream

Another amazing innovation from Renew World Outreach is the LightStream portable media device. By creating its own local WiFi network, LightStream allows nearby smartphones to stream or download stored media through an intuitive interface. It also facilitates the copying of entire media libraries onto microSD cards that can be shared from device to device.[7]

LightStream can be a powerful tool for anonymous evangelism in closed countries. Imagine a young believer in a closed country—maybe Pakistan or Indonesia. She walks into a coffee shop, orders, and begins to enjoy her drink. She casually reaches into her bag and powers on her LightStream. Within minutes, a Wi-Fi network comes to life. Curious patrons check their phones and discover a new network. Some tap in, finding a library of Bible stories, worship music, and *The JESUS Film*. A young man in the corner, who has been searching for hope, presses play. No one speaks a word, but the gospel is moving, unseen.

RADIO AND TV MINISTRIES

Radio and television ministries have long been mainstays in the effort to reach the unreached. Ministries in this space are sending God's Word through the air into places missionaries cannot easily go.

The Power of Radio

Radio's simplicity and accessibility make it a powerful tool for the gospel, particularly in regions where infrastructure is limited. A small, battery-powered radio can bring the gospel to remote places where infrastructure and literacy are lacking.

One of the leading radio ministries is Trans World Radio (TWR). Since its founding in 1954, TWR has shared the gospel across six continents and in more than 275 languages, reaching an estimated 4 billion people worldwide each year.[8] In places like North Africa, where evangelism is illegal, TWR programs offer hope to listeners in their heart languages. A man in Algeria wrote, "Your programs are like water in the desert. They give life to my soul."

> Radio's simplicity and accessibility make it a powerful tool for the gospel.

Another leading radio ministry is Far East Broadcasting Company (FEBC), which has been broadcasting the gospel since 1945. FEBC focuses on Asia, Africa, and the Middle East, using short-wave, AM/FM, and Internet radio to reach millions. In Cambodia, FEBC's broadcasts in the Khmer language have faithfully shared the gospel through decades of war and persecution. One listener shared, "Through the radio, I met Jesus. His words gave me hope when everything seemed lost."

Television: Bringing Jesus into Living Rooms

One of the most impactful television ministries is SAT-7, a Christian satellite network broadcasting into the Middle East and North Africa. SAT-7 produces programs in Arabic, Farsi, and Turkish, designed to share the gospel and disciple believers in a culturally sensitive way. In Iran, where owning a Bible can lead to imprisonment, believers gather in secret to watch SAT-7 broadcasts. Viewers write in, saying, "Your programs are my church. I have no other way to learn about Jesus." SAT-7 estimates that over 25 million people watch their broadcasts every year.[9]

In India, ministries like Gospel for Asia use television to reach people in both rural and urban areas. Programs featuring testimonies, Bible teaching, and music are broadcast in English and local languages.

Breaking Barriers: Media in Restricted Nations

One of the greatest strengths of radio and television is their ability to penetrate regions closed to traditional missions. For example, FEBC and TWR broadcast Christian programming into North Korea through powerful shortwave signals. North Koreans who secretly tune in to these broadcasts often risk their lives to hear the message of Jesus. One listener wrote, "In this dark place, your programs give me light and courage to keep going."

One striking example of technology's impact on evangelism is the growth of the church in Iran. Despite intense persecution,

A SPY COMES TO CHRIST

Ahmad is an online discipler who used the Safar app from Elam Ministries to disciple Adel, a new believer in Iran.

Late one night after they had met, Adel called back, crying. Through his tears, he said, "I lied to you. I am a spy for the security police. But today, I really want to give my heart to Jesus." He asked, "Brother, can we start Safar again, from step one?"

Safar step eight is about sharing the gospel with others. After the lesson, Adel talked with his wife about Jesus. Three days later, she came to faith. Two days after that, his daughter received Christ. Two weeks later, his niece believed.

With Adel's family coming to Christ, Ahmad invited him for training on leading weekly fellowships. There he met other believers who prayed with him and encouraged him. He returned to Iran stronger.

Adel wanted to start a fellowship, but he knew his home would not be safe. Instead, he proposed a most unlikely location: the home of his devout Muslim parents. They reluctantly allowed the fellowship to meet in their home. Each week, they would sit in a corner and listen. But as they heard God being worshiped in Persian and not Arabic, they were drawn in.

One night, after the gathering, they had questions for Adel. After taking in his answers, his father jumped up and shouted, "Jesus Christ is Lord!" His mother also gave her life to Christ.

The weekly fellowship continues to meet and has now grown to nine people. Ahmad continues to lead Adel as he leads others.

Christianity is flourishing, largely due to media. Online platforms, satellite TV, and messaging apps are fueling the fastest-growing underground church movement in the world. Ministries report that over a million Iranians have come to faith in Christ in recent years, with much of this growth attributed to technology-driven outreach.

One striking example of technology's impact on evangelism is the growth of the church in Iran.

Elam Ministries' mission is to strengthen and expand the church in Iran and beyond. Because traditional ministry methods are dangerous in Iran, Elam uses creative and secure digital strategies. Their Safar journey is a step-by-step discipleship tool that helps new believers learn how to know and follow Jesus and become disciple makers. The Kalameh app helps small groups of believers engage together with God's Word, worship, prayer, and mission. Using these proven tools, Elam is mobilizing Iranians around the world to reach out to family and friends back home.

CONCLUSION

The numbers speak for themselves. Through technology and media—radio, TV, films, audio Bibles, and the Internet—billions of people have encountered the gospel. These tools are bridging gaps that were once insurmountable, reaching people in their heart languages, and enabling discipleship in ways that were unimaginable a few decades ago.

I have highlighted a dozen ministries in this chapter, but there are many others that are harnessing technology to make disciples of Jesus. As technology advances, its impact will only grow. More programs will be produced. More language groups will be reached. And more people will hear the name of Jesus. The gospel is going forth electronically, carrying with it the promise of Matthew 24:14: "And this gospel of the kingdom will be preached in the whole world as a testimony to all nations, and then the end will come."

CHAPTER 11

The Foundation of Prayer

Although Jesus gave the church the responsibility for taking the good news to the whole world, accomplishing that task is far beyond our natural ability. On our own we are weak and ineffective, and the forces that oppose us are far stronger than we are. The world, the devil, and sinful human nature all are opposed to the gospel, and any effort to rescue people from Satan's kingdom of darkness will be challenged. The battle can only be won through the spiritual power and authority of Christ.

Thankfully, Jesus has been given "all authority in heaven and on earth" and has promised, "I am with you always." But to be victorious, we must engage his power and presence, which we do through prayer. And that is why prayer is the foundation for all other Great Commission work.

JESUS MODELED PRAYER

Jesus made this clear in Luke 10:2. Before he sent out the seventy-two, "He told them, 'The harvest is plentiful, but the workers are few. Ask the Lord of the harvest, therefore, to send out workers into his harvest field.'" The first step in the harvest is always prayer.

Of course, Jesus modeled the importance and power of prayer personally. Luke tells us, "Jesus often withdrew to lonely places and prayed" (Luke 5:16). Mark records, "Very early in the morning, while it was still dark, Jesus got up, left the house and went off to a solitary place, where he prayed" (Mark 1:35). For Jesus, prayer wasn't occasional or optional but a priority. It was the rhythm of his life.

More than that, though, prayer was the source of Jesus' power. He said, "Very truly I tell you, the Son can do nothing by himself; he can do only what he sees his Father doing" (John 5:19). Before choosing the twelve disciples, "Jesus went out to a mountainside to pray, and spent the night praying to God" (Luke 6:12). He prayed before Peter's confession (Luke 9:18), before his transfiguration (Luke 9:28), and in agony in Gethsemane, saying, "Abba, Father . . . not what I will, but what you will" (Mark 14:36).

> Prayer is the foundation for all other Great Commission work.

Jesus' life was a constant expression of dependence on the Father. And if the Son depended completely on the Father in everything, how much more must we?

WE MUST PRAY

Jesus emphasized dependence when he declared, "apart from me you can do nothing" (John 15:5). Only when we abide in him—which requires, among other things, continual prayer—can we accomplish anything of spiritual significance.

The other New Testament writers also stress the critical role of prayer. Paul commanded believers to "pray continually" (1 Thessalonians 5:17). James wrote, "The prayer of a righteous person is powerful and effective" (James 5:16), highlighting prayer as a source of transformational power. Jude called believers to build "yourselves up in your most holy faith and [pray] in the Holy Spirit" (Jude 1:20).

Jesus specifically instructed us to pray for the Great Commission. In fact, prayer for the Great Commission is embedded in the Lord's Prayer: "Our Father in heaven, hallowed be your name, your kingdom come, your will be done, on earth as it is in heaven . . ." What is the Great Commission other than extending God's sovereignty to the ends of the earth?

The Lausanne Movement has long affirmed that mission efforts without prayer are ineffective. In their foundational paper, *Prayer in Evangelism*, they emphasize that prayer must undergird every evangelistic endeavor. It says, "Prayer is fundamental to evangelism . . . because the work of redemption is the work of God. Prayer acknowledges God's primacy . . . and fulfils God's command that Christians ask him to act."[1] In other words, the Great Commission is a spiritual battle, and it must be fought with spiritual weapons.

I've frequently told my Finishing Fund colleagues that apart from God's blessing, all our efforts amount to five loaves and two fish—completely inadequate to the task at hand. We work hard and strive to do our best, but it is only when Jesus blesses our work that it becomes sufficient to make an eternal impact. I love how

Moses expressed this same utter dependence in Exodus 33:15: "If your Presence does not go with us, do not send us up from here."

"Prayer does not fit us for the greater works; prayer is the greater work."

He knew that without the empowering presence of God, the Israelites would never be able to do what he had called them to do.

Oswald Chambers famously wrote, "Prayer does not fit us for the greater works; prayer is the greater work."[2] We tend to think of prayer as the preparation for tasks like evangelism, church planting, or translation—a bit like stretching or taping up before playing a basketball game. Chambers' point is that prayer isn't the preparation but the work itself. Equipped through prayer with Jesus' authority and presence, we cannot be stopped; without it, we might as well not even try.

MINISTRY PRAYER

Every Great Commission ministry I know of agrees with that, and all of them have extensive prayer undergirding everything they do. Let's look at a few examples.

The Timothy Initiative (TTI)

Every aspect of The Timothy Initiative's work is undergirded by prayer, beginning with its 24/7 global prayer movement. Supporters can sign up for one or more 15-minute slots at TTIPray.org.

The TTI team in each country has its own rhythm of prayer. In India, for example, the central office begins every workday with forty-five to sixty minutes of devotion, worship, Scripture, and focused intercession. Once a month, the team devotes an entire day to fasting and prayer. Smaller prayer clusters spring up spontaneously throughout the week. Regional offices follow the same pattern, beginning each day with intercession for the unreached.

Before launching any new project, the entire team of staff and field leaders commit to a twenty-four-hour chain of prayer that can last for months. Ahead of each quarterly training, each member of the team—from national leaders down to newly trained Tituses—commits to at least one hour of prayer, ensuring that at least one person is always praying for forty straight days. Additional "prayer fuel" gatherings target urgent needs—persecution, local opposition, or national emergencies.

For TTI, prayer is not incidental to the mission but is its power. Their intentional rhythms of prayer sustain workers, propel the harvest, and make space for God to move in miraculous ways.

unfoldingWord

The pattern is similar at unfoldingWord, a leading Church-Centric Bible Translation ministry. Every Monday morning, their full staff meets online for prayer. After a short time together on Zoom, they break into smaller groups who pray for an hour. Every Thursday they hold a prayer meeting focused entirely on field partners. Prayer needs are tracked and shared using two digital information boards: one for internal requests and another, secure board for field partner needs.

In addition to these weekly rhythms, once every month there is a Global Prayer Zoom call that includes international partners from around the world.

Beyond these internal disciplines, unfoldingWord collaborates with broader prayer movements in Bible translation. The ministry is an active part of the Every Tribe Every Nation (ETEN) and illumi-*Nations* prayer strategy working group, helping to lead monthly intercession efforts and contributing prayer leadership at events like the ETEN Summit and Illumi*Nations* gathering.

Team Expansion

Team Expansion was born out of extraordinary prayer in a Kentucky college dorm room in 1978, and prayer remains foundational to all their work. They believe that God moves in response to prayer for peoples and places, opening doors for new fields and disciple-making efforts.

During the first thirty minutes of every workday, staff from around the world pray together for one part of the world, asking for more harvest workers, for favor with government leaders, and for missionaries in the specified countries. Once a week, the International Services staff gathers to pray for every one of the ministry's field workers by name. Each month, the entire staff meets for half a day for fasting, praise, thanksgiving, and petition with focus on one of Team Expansion's twelve missionary fields.

> *Every Great Commission ministry I know of has extensive prayer undergirding everything they do.*

In addition to that rhythm, over the years Team Expansion has hosted Great Commission prayer events for nearby churches.

GREAT COMMISSION PRAYER INITIATIVES

Great Commission prayer initiatives mobilize the global church to intercede for the fulfillment of the Great Commission. Whether through 24/7 prayer chains, national fasting movements, or local church gatherings, these initiatives serve as spiritual engines behind the global missions movement.

International Prayer Connect (IPC)

International Prayer Connect is a global coalition of over 5,000 prayer networks and organizations committed to seeing every nation transformed through united prayer. Founded by John Robb and now led by Dr. Jason Hubbard, IPC believes that prayer is foundational to the Great Commission task. As Dr. Hubbard often says, "God releases his power in response to the prayers of his people."

In 2022, IPC launched the 110 Cities Prayer Initiative in partnership with Finishing the Task. It targets 110 of the world's largest urban centers—cities like Mumbai, London, and Lagos—for ongoing 24/7 prayer. Due to migration and urbanization, at least 90 percent of the world's unreached people groups can be found in these cities. They are also spiritual and cultural centers for their countries. The initiative aims to recruit 110 million believers to pray for these cities at least four times a year on IPC's Global Days of Prayer. Participants can choose to pray for a particular city or to receive emails that highlight different cities.

> IPC's 110 Cities Prayer Initiative targets 110 of the world's largest urban centers for ongoing 24/7 prayer.

As of 2023, more than 100 million believers have taken part, committing a total of 2,192 days of prayer. Eighty-six of the 110 cities have strong indigenous prayer movements, and many of them now have uninterrupted, round-the-clock prayer.

Each of IPC's Global Days of Prayer focuses on a single world religion and is timed to coincide with a spiritually significant date. In 2026, the planned dates are:

- Chinese New Year, February 17, for the Buddhist world
- Laylat al-Qadr (the holiest night of the year in Islam), March 17
- Pentecost, May 24, for Judaism
- Diwali (the Hindu holiday celebrating the triumph of light over darkness), November 8

IPC also partners with illumi*Nations* in the Pray for Zero initiative, aiming for zero Bibleless languages by 2033. Through this effort, intercessors are mobilized to cover every Scripture translation project in prayer.

Pray for All

Pray for All is a bold initiative to pray for each person on Earth by name by Pentecost 2033, in keeping with the command of 1 Timothy 2:1: "I urge, then, first of all, that petitions, prayers, intercession and thanksgiving be made for *all people.*"

The movement began after a 2019 meeting between Brian Alarid, founder of America Prays and World Prays, and Mark Anderson, founder of Call2All. Recognizing the enormity of the task, Alarid gathered a coalition that now includes Finishing the Task, IPC, Cru, Every Home for Christ, and Empowered21. The work is advancing through regional hubs across six continents. Local churches and ministries are mapping homes, gathering names, and assigning intercessors to pray personally for each person. Pray for All offers a mobile app that provides reminders and resources to support those who commit to pray. To date, more than 500 million people have already been prayed for by name.

Brian Alarid's book, *By Name: How to Pray for People and Lead Them to Jesus*, outlines five lifestyle habits modeled by Jesus: pray, listen, eat, serve, and share. The book aims to equip readers to love people like Jesus and impact their communities for eternity.

Prayercast

A ministry of OneWay, Prayercast uses media to ignite global intercession. Its library of video prayers—many narrated by indigenous believers—covers every nation, religion, and issue and is used by churches, missions agencies, and individuals in over 180 countries. Special initiatives like Love Muslims during Ramadan and the World Religions Prayer Plan help guide focused intercession. Prayercast also equips believers through educational resources, reinforcing the truth that prayer is the first act of mission.

Other Global Prayer Movements

There are numerous other initiatives mobilizing prayer for the unreached and the Great Commission. Praying Through the Window focuses on the 10/40 Window—the region from North Africa around to Indonesia that is home to most of the world's unreached peoples. The website WIN1040.org offers focused prayer guides for each 10/40 country.

The Ethne Prayer Initiative organizes monthly prayers for the world's least-reached frontier people groups, mobilizing intercessors to lift up specific ethnic groups with little or no access to the gospel. Prayer guides and regular updates help believers pray strategically for breakthroughs in the hardest places.

The 30 Days of Prayer for the Muslim World began in 1993 and has since mobilized millions of Christians each year to pray during the Islamic month of Ramadan (February 18 through March 19 in 2026). Each day focuses on a different aspect of the Muslim world—its people, beliefs, and challenges—encouraging informed, loving intercession. This initiative has helped fuel the explosion of spiritual hunger across the Islamic world.

24-7 Prayer International is a global, interdenominational movement calling people to seek God through nonstop prayer, mission, and justice. What began in 1999 as a student-led prayer room in England—inspired by the Moravians' century-long prayer vigil—has now spread to more than half the nations on Earth, with over 25,000 prayer rooms established. The movement also equips believers through resources like The Prayer Course and the Lectio 365 app.

Global Prayer Resource Network (GlobalPRN) is a one-stop source offering links to many other prayer ministries and efforts. It offers practical tools like downloadable prayer guides, worship-based Scripture readings, and models for 24/7 prayer to deepen and sustain targeted intercession.

RESOURCES FOR PRAYER

In addition to these initiatives, many ministries offer resources that help guide prayer for the Great Commission. Operation World (OW) publishes in-depth, country-by-country prayer profiles that equip believers to pray strategically for the nations. First published in 1974 by Patrick Johnstone, today OW produces a comprehensive reference book, digital resource, and mobile app, in multiple languages. These are used by churches, mission agencies, and individual believers to fuel informed, worldwide prayer.

The Joshua Project provides daily prayer profiles through its Unreached of the Day app, podcasts, and printable PDFs, making it easy to pray for a new unreached people group each day. Each profile includes key information— language, location, religion, population, and gospel status—along with specific prayer points.

PeopleGroups.org, a ministry of the International Mission Board (IMB), focuses specifically on unengaged unreached people groups (UUPGs). The site offers

In every hard place where the gospel is advancing, prayer has gone ahead to prepare the way.

a variety of tools to guide prayer, including downloadable prayer cards and PrayerThreads, a resource designed to unite believers in focused intercession around common gospel barriers.

Finally, it's worth mentioning a couple of great books that have helped me develop a better prayer life. One is *A Praying Life* by Paul Miller, a deeply practical and personal book that helps believers cultivate a rich, honest, and persistent prayer life rooted in relationship with God. Another is *Lead with Prayer* by Ryan Skoog, Peter Greer, and Cameron Doolittle. *Lead with Prayer* explores the prayer habits of impactful Christian leaders and invites readers into a deeper life of intimacy with God.

CONCLUSION

These movements of prayer are not perfunctory—they have power, and they're bearing fruit. Missionaries testify that prayer opens hearts, protects teams, and disarms spiritual strongholds. In closed nations, reports of dreams, visions, and divine encounters often follow seasons of intense global prayer. Church-planting movements in places like Iran, India, and North Africa frequently trace their origins to focused intercession. In every hard place where the gospel is advancing, prayer has gone ahead to prepare the way.

The task is enormous, but prayer unlocks the power and presence of Christ to accomplish what otherwise would be impossible. More people praying and more prayers going out will drive us closer to the three "every" finish lines.

And the best news is that praying is one part of the task that everyone can do. So if you're not already praying for the Great Commission, commit right now to do so—and join the sprint to the finish of the Great Commission race.

CHAPTER 12

The Reality of Opposition

The Great Commission is a war between two great kingdoms: the kingdom of darkness, which once ruled the entire world, and the Kingdom of God, which is overthrowing it. God's Kingdom advances through spiritual battles—for individuals, people groups, and even countries. Every time the gospel is preached in a place where Christ is not yet named, it confronts the powers of darkness head-on.

Satan knows what is at stake. He understands that his days are numbered. So he resists the Great Commission with everything he has—deception, distraction, discouragement, violence, and fear. He does not give up territory easily. Wherever the church moves forward in mission, the enemy pushes back with force.

JESUS' WARNINGS

Jesus warned about this from the beginning, preparing his disciples for what they would face as the message moved out from Jerusalem. He sent his disciples out, not with promises of comfort and ease, but with sober cautions: "I am sending you out like sheep among wolves," he told them (Matthew 10:16). "If they persecuted me," he said, "they will persecute you also" (John 15:20). Jesus warned of arrests, floggings, betrayals, and executions—because he knew that the message of the kingdom would provoke fierce opposition. "They will deliver you over to courts," He said, "and flog you in their synagogues, and you will be dragged before governors and kings for my sake" (Matthew 10:17–18, ESV). It wasn't theoretical. Persecution was the job description for those who would take the gospel to the nations.

THE APOSTLES: A PATTERN OF SUFFERING

Almost right away, Jesus' warnings came true. Peter and John were seized, jailed, and brought before the Sanhedrin (the Jewish ruling council), who commanded them not to preach in the name of Jesus (Acts 4). A little while later, Peter and the apostles were arrested for preaching the gospel. When they were miraculously released and returned to preaching, they were brought before the Sanhedrin again, who warned them again and had them flogged. Acts 5:41 says

The Great Commission is a war between two great kingdoms.

that the apostles "left the Sanhedrin, rejoicing because they had been counted worthy of suffering disgrace for the Name." That joyful defiance in the face of persecution has remained the spirit of the Great Commission right down to today.

SAMI

Sami came from a devout Muslim family in West Africa. As a young man, he worked in a nearby country. His desire was to make money, and he lived for his own pleasure.

Even though it was illegal there to evangelize, a Christian neighbor faithfully shared with him about Jesus and the good news. After some time, Sami received Christ, and his life was radically changed. He joined a ministry and began building relationships with Muslims and telling them about Jesus.

One day when Sami was returning from ministry in a nearby village, his motorbike was hit by a car, and he was killed. The car was driven by Sami's landlord, who knew Sami to be a Christian. Was he hit intentionally? There is no way to know. Because Sami was a Christian, and his landlord had government ties, there was no investigation.

Sami was buried by fellow Christians—in a Muslim graveyard, since there was no Christian cemetery in the city. They paid the burial fees and held a quiet memorial service.

Over the next few days, imams in the city began protesting, upset that a Christian had been given a proper burial. The protests erupted into riots, and five days later, some men dug up Sami's body. Hundreds cheered them on. His body was then dragged through the city to make an example of what is done to "infidels."

Since then, several Christians have had to relocate due to increased security risks. They have not stopped their work, but it is hindered by the threat of violence.

Later, Stephen—one of the deacons of the Jerusalem church—was seized and brought before religious leaders. When he condemned them, they dragged him outside the city and stoned him to death while he prayed for their forgiveness (Acts 7:59–60). His death unleashed a wave of persecution in Jerusalem. "On that day," Luke writes, "a great persecution broke out against the church," and believers were scattered throughout Judea and Samaria (Acts 8:1).

But as we saw in chapter 10, that scattering advanced the mission. "Those who had been scattered preached the word wherever they went" (Acts 8:4). That pattern has also continued until today—persecution and opposition often accelerate the spread of the faith.

In Acts 12 we read about the martyrdom of James, the brother of Jesus and the leader of the Jerusalem church. Herod Agrippa had him "put to death with the sword," likely by beheading. When that brought favor from the Jews, Herod also had Peter arrested, and planned to kill him as well. But God arranged a miraculous escape. Again, this is a pattern that has continued through history: God (sometimes) acting miraculously to rescue his people.

The apostle Paul also faced enormous opposition. In 2 Corinthians 11, Paul catalogs his sufferings: five times whipped with thirty-nine lashes, three times beaten with rods, once stoned and left for dead. He was shipwrecked, imprisoned, starved, and constantly in danger: "In danger from rivers, in danger from bandits, in danger from my fellow Jews, in danger from Gentiles . . . in danger in the city, in danger in the country, in danger at sea" (2 Corinthians 11:26). The man who brought the gospel to the Gentiles did so at *enormous* personal cost. Ultimately, Paul was imprisoned in Rome for two years, then released, only later to be imprisoned again and finally martyred by Nero in about 67 AD.

As we saw in Chapter 4, the other apostles suffered similarly. All but John are thought to have given their lives for the spread of the gospel.

THE BLOOD OF THE MARTYRS

Tertullian, a North African church father in the second century, said, "The blood of the martyrs is the seed of the church." History has proven him right.

Tens of thousands of Christian converts were martyred in Persia in the fourth century during the reign of Shapur II.[1]

In the fifth century, Patrick faced violent threats from tribal chieftains and opposition from powerful druid priests in Ireland.[2]

In 754, Boniface was martyred by a pagan mob in Frisia.[3]

> The blood of the martyrs is the seed of the church.

Adalbert of Prague, a tenth century missionary to the Slavic and Baltic peoples, was martyred by pagan warriors in Prussia in 997.[4]

Berard of Carbio and four others were sent by Francis of Assisi as missionaries to Morocco. In 1220, they were beaten and beheaded.[5]

ACHMED

Achmed lives in one of the world's most restrictive countries, where the constitution requires every citizen to be a Muslim and Christianity is punishable by death. Until recently, there were no known Christians in the country.

Achmed became a believer when Salim—perhaps the first Christian in the country, and the only Fulani Christian Achmed had ever seen—led him to Christ. Achmed had seen *The JESUS Film* and had even dreamed of Jesus. But only when Salim explained the gospel did it all make sense.

At first, Achmed kept his faith secret, but gradually he began telling others—first his family and eventually many friends. All the while, his career advanced, and he moved in the highest circles of power.

But one day, a video of Achmed baptizing a man surfaced on social media, sparking outrage among the Muslims. Knowing what might be coming, Achmed and the small group of believers gathered. What should they do? Many advised them to hide or to flee, but they decided to stay and trust God.

Soon after, police raided Achmed's home. When they questioned him, he admitted that he was a Christian. They arrested him, along with his friend Mustafa and Achmed's brother. Over the next few days, a total of twenty-three believers were seized.

When Salim heard of the arrests, he wrote to his American missionary friend, If the children are struck, the father must appear. Please pray for me." Day after day, he risked life and freedom to visit his friends in jail.

Over and over, the authorities threatened the men and demanded that they recant. Under growing pressure, seven believers folded. But the rest continued to affirm their faith.

A few days later, they were taken before the nation's top prosecutor—a man Achmed knew. "The accusations against you are very serious. Why destroy your life? Just confess Mohammed and you'll be free." Achmed replied, "I cannot. The accusations are true. I follow Jesus."

Three days later, there was a trial. The judge warned Achmed that apostasy carries the death penalty. Still, he refused to renounce Christ. The judge stared at him in amazement. When Mustafa did the same, the judge stopped calling the cases, unsure what to do. Were they all willing to die?

Several former colleagues came to persuade Achmed. He was offered money and promised a better job if he would just say the words. His sister came, sobbing, and threatened to kill herself. He gently told her he could not recant.

And then, miraculously, they were all released. The men were amazed—nothing like this had every happened in their country. They left prison rejoicing and praising God for his miraculous rescue.

Their story swept the nation. Some were outraged, but others were drawn by the believers' astounding faith. Achmed is still in danger, and he has lost his prestigious position. But he continues to share his faith fearlessly, and the church in their country is growing rapidly.

In 1315, Raymond Lull, a Franciscan missionary to Muslims in North Africa, was stoned to death by a hostile crowd.[6]

William Tyndale was strangled and burned at the stake in 1536. His crime? Translating the Bible into English.[7]

In 1597, the 26 Martyrs of Nagasaki—six European missionaries and 20 Japanese converts—were crucified on a hillside overlooking the city.[8]

In 1732, Johann Leonhard Dober and David Nitschmann faced violent opposition from colonial authorities and plantation owners who beat, jailed, and tried to expel them. [9]

In the nineteenth century, Adoniram Judson endured imprisonment, disease, and the death of two wives and several children in Burma. [10]

In China, dozens of China Inland Mission missionaries were killed during the Boxer Rebellion of 1900.[11]

In 1956, Jim Elliot and four others were speared to death by members of the Waorani tribe in Ecuador. [12]

These are but a few of the thousands of stories of persecution and martyrdom faced by faithful men and women pursuing Jesus' "every nation, every language, every place" commands. Suffering is not the exception but the rule—the common experience of God's messengers throughout history.

TODAY

Persecution is not just a story of the past. It is the present reality in much of the world today. Around the world, missionaries and converts face harassment, arrest, beatings, and death for daring to obey Christ.

Missionary John Chau was killed in 2018 when he tried to take the gospel to the unengaged people of North Sentinel Island.

In many parts of in India, Hindu extremists violently oppose gospel workers. Evangelists are routinely attacked by mobs, churches burned, and converts threatened or expelled from their villages. In 2008, more than 100 Christians were killed in the Kandhamal district of Odisha during an anti-Christian riot that specifically targeted missionaries and church leaders.[13] In 2023, more than 600 incidents of violence against Christians were reported in India, many aimed at those involved in church-planting efforts.[14]

> *Suffering and persecution are not the exception but the rule—the common experience of God's messengers.*

The Indian government has imposed severe restrictions on fund flows in an effort to starve out missions efforts. As a result, more than 10,000 NGOs—many of them Christian missionary organizations—have lost their licenses to receive foreign funds, leading many to cease operations in India.[15]

The government of Iran sees evangelism as a threat to Islamic identity. House church leaders and Christian converts are routinely

KIBIR

On a hot summer evening in central India, a mob of eighteen men arrived at Kibir's house. Kibir, a new follower of Jesus, had opened his home for a gathering of new believers in his humble village. They had met Christ through the witness of men who had come to share the faith and plant churches.

Seeing the gathering, the mob pushed in, swinging sticks. They beat Kibir until he was unconscious and drove his guests away. His home was destroyed, and friends and family were left in shock.

Prior to being taken to the hospital, Kibir was carried to the police station and charged with "attempting to convert people to Christianity"—a serious violation of India's strict anti-conversion laws. The police demanded that he sign a statement renouncing Christianity and agreeing that he and his family would return to their Hindu roots. When he refused, he and his family were banished from their home and village to be made an example to the community of what happens to those who seek to leave Hinduism.

Kibir and his family are now living with another family in a distant village. He is recovering from his beating. He remains a follower of Jesus.

arrested. Missionaries caught sharing the gospel are often sentenced as national security threats.

Yousef Nadarkhani, a former Muslim who became a Christian at 19, served as a pastor in Iran's underground house church movement and was known for his bold witness and refusal to compromise his faith. He spent years in prison, receiving a death sentence for apostasy and later a ten-year sentence for "acting against national security," all for the simple act of following and preaching Christ.[16]

North Korea is one of the most dangerous places in the world for Christians. Missionaries and gospel workers have been detained, tortured, and executed. In 2013, Korean-American missionary Kenneth Bae was arrested and sentenced to fifteen years of hard labor for "hostile acts," which included preaching the gospel. Others have simply disappeared.[17]

Evangelism in Somalia is punishable by death. Maxamed Xuseen Axmed, one of the first known Somali believers, was kidnapped and martyred on April 3, 1996—one of six to be killed for their faith in the first few months of that year. Even today converts face execution by extremist groups. Foreign mission workers cannot operate openly; they are marked for deportations or even death if discovered.[18]

Sometimes called "the North Korea of Africa," Eritrea imprisons Christian leaders and missionaries indefinitely without trial. Many have been held for years in shipping containers, subjected to extreme heat and cold. Preaching the gospel outside of state-sanctioned churches is considered treasonous.[19]

Missionaries in northern Nigeria live under constant threat from Boko Haram and Fulani extremists. Churches have been bombed, pastors executed, and whole villages razed. In 2021, Pastor Bulus Yakuru was abducted and later killed after refusing to renounce his faith.[20]

In communist Laos, Christianity is viewed with deep suspicion. Sharing the gospel without government approval is illegal, and house churches are often raided by police. Evangelists have been arrested, interrogated, and imprisoned for "disrupting national unity." In some remote provinces, Christian converts have been expelled from their villages or denied access to water and food unless they renounce their faith. Yet the underground church continues to grow.[21]

The government of China has intensified its crackdown on both missionaries and local gospel movements. Most Western missionaries have been expelled. House church leaders have been arrested, church buildings demolished, and Christian literature confiscated. Some pastors have disappeared, and families have been pressured to deny Christ in exchange for jobs, education, or basic services.[22]

And this is just a partial list. The World Evangelical Alliance estimates that over 300 million Christians today live under some form of persecution—many of them in places where mission efforts are advancing most rapidly.[23]

WHY?

Why would Christ—who has all authority in heaven and on earth—allow his messengers to suffer like this? If he wanted, he could silence every oppressor, deflect every bullet, and shield every missionary from harm. And one day he will. But for now, he permits his servants to suffer because he is accomplishing something greater through their suffering than he would through their safety. The gospel is a message of sacrifice, and it is often most powerful when carried by people who are willing to suffer for it.

Persecution purifies the church. It strips away comfort, pride, and pretense. When following Jesus is risky, only those who truly

SOKHA SANN

Sokha Sann was a subsistence farmer in a Southeast Asian country. Like many in his country, he was an animist who worshipped the spirits.

But in 2015 Sokha's entire family became Christians. He began to lead Sunday gatherings for a few believers in his home.

Opposition came quickly. Village leaders considered Sokha's faith incompatible with their traditions. The believers were ostracized, denied access to the village well, and threatened.

In 2018, Sokha was arrested. Officials pressed him to recant, but he refused. He was detained for three days and released only after his family paid a "service fee."

Even so, Sokha continued leading the church. He also helped launch a new church in a nearby village and began hosting movement training—despite repeated warnings.

Late in 2022, Sokha set out to meet with some Christian leaders. He called his wife to say he had safely crossed the mountain pass. But he never arrived. The next morning, a witness reported seeing three men force him into a black truck. The police found his motorbike abandoned on the road.

Two days later, his body was found. He had been tortured: There were stab wounds, burns, a gash above his right eye, and numerous bruises. Police opened an investigation but seemed unconcerned about finding the killers. The believers know that is because Sokha was killed for his faith—probably by the local or district authorities.

believe will follow. That kind of faith—refined by the fire of hardship—is not only a witness to the world but a weapon against the enemy. Jesus said, "Blessed are you when people insult you, persecute you and falsely say all kinds of evil against you because of me . . . for great is your reward in heaven" (Matthew 5:11–12). That reward is not only future—it bears fruit now, as the world watches and wonders what kind of Savior merits such loyalty.

Suffering also expands the mission. Though it looks like defeat, God uses it to scatter seed. After Stephen was stoned, the church in Jerusalem was forced out—but they preached the Word wherever they went (Acts 8:4). Paul's prison letters have discipled hundreds of millions of believers through the centuries. Again and again, martyrdom becomes the soil from which movements grow. History has proven Tertullian's statement true.

Jesus permits his servants to suffer because he is accomplishing something greater through their suffering than he would through their safety.

Above all, suffering for the gospel brings us into deeper fellowship with Christ himself. He was hated, opposed, beaten, and crucified. When we suffer for his name, it is not because He has abandoned us but because He is inviting us into deeper intimacy with him. "I want to know Christ," Paul wrote, "I want to suffer with him, sharing in his death" (Philippians 3:10 ESV). Jesus allows us to share in his suffering so that we may also share in his glory. And through that suffering, his power is made perfect, his gospel is magnified, and his kingdom marches forward, unstoppable.

VICTORY IS CERTAIN

Despite all of this, the victory is certain. The suffering is real—but so is the power of Christ. He has declared that "this gospel of the kingdom *will be* preached in the whole world" and that "You *will be* my witnesses . . . to the ends of the earth." Not *might be* or *may be* or *could be* or *should be* but *will be*. He has promised it, and it will happen. Despite the best efforts of the enemy to thwart God's plans and our efforts, one day soon there *will be* disciples in every nation; Jesus *will be* praised in every language; and the good news *will be* preached in the whole world. Jesus' promises are certain. The sacrifices of the martyrs have not been in vain. The Great Commission will be finished, and the kingdom of darkness will fall.

CHAPTER 13

Finding Your Lane

Second Peter chapter 3 is all about the end times. Peter begins by reminding his readers of the many prophecies about things to come and warns that in the last days "scoffers will come" asking "where is this 'coming' he promised." He assures them that judgment is surely coming and that the "Lord is not slow in keeping his promise" but "patient with you, not wanting anyone to perish, but everyone to come to repentance."

Having set the stage, he then asks and answers an important question: "Since everything will be destroyed in this way, what kind of people ought you to be? You ought to live holy and godly lives as you look forward to the day of God and speed its coming" (2 Peter 3:11–12).

In light of the coming judgment, Peter asks, how should we live? First, he says, we must live holy and godly lives. That shouldn't be surprising. The Bible repeatedly commands us to be holy and encourages us to live Godly lives, and serious believers do our best to live up to those lofty aspirations. The word *holy* means "set apart," so Peter is calling for God's people to be different, separate, and distinct from the world. *Godly* means "like God," and thankfully, we have a perfect illustration of what that looks like in Jesus. If we want to be like God, we should strive to be like Jesus, increasingly displaying the fruit of the Spirit.

Peter also says that we should "look forward to the day of God." In other words, we should live in anticipation and excitement about the return of Christ and the establishment of his kingdom. If this was Peter's command 2,000 years ago, how much more relevant is it today, when it's possible we will see God's Kingdom come in our lifetimes?

One aspect of "looking forward" to that day is to be awake and aware of the times in which we live (1 Thessalonians 5:2–6; Revelation 3:3). That's why I've written this book: to inform you about the amazing things God is doing to complete the Great Commission and to alert you to the implications of its completion—the coming of the day of God.

But then Peter says something surprising: We shouldn't just *look forward* to that day, but we should *speed its coming*. The Good News Translation says we should "do [our] best to make it come soon" and the ESV says we ought to be "hastening the coming of the day of God" (2 Peter 3:12).

But how can we do that? How is it possible for any of us to do anything to hasten the coming of Jesus? Doesn't God set that date, and hasn't it already been set?

Throughout this book we've talked about the link between the completion of the Great Commission and the return of Christ. We've said that Jesus commanded his church to take the good news to every people group, every language, and every place and said that he would not come back before that task was completed. If that's correct, there is one thing that each of us can do to hasten Jesus' coming—accelerate the completion of the Great Commission.

But what is your part? What lane has God called you to fill in the sprint to the finish of the Great Commission Race?

WHAT'S MY LANE?

One of my favorite Bible verses is Ephesians 2:10. Most believers know the two immediately preceding verses, which say "it is by grace you have been saved, through faith—and this is not from yourselves, it is the gift of God—not by works, so that no one can boast." Those verses teach that salvation is a gift, received by grace through faith, and has absolutely nothing to do with our works.

But then, in the very next verse, Paul says, "For we are God's handiwork, created in Christ Jesus to do good works, which God prepared in advance for us to do." Each of us has been "created in Christ Jesus" for the explicit purpose of doing good works— tasks that God has "prepared in advance" specifically and individually for each of us. So while works

> Each of us has been "created in Christ Jesus" for the explicit purpose of doing good works.

have nothing to do with our salvation, they have *everything* to do with our lives as believers.

I am intrigued by the vivid contrast between these ideas: saved apart from works for the purpose of doing works. I love the idea that God has a plan for my life—that he has prepared good works particularly for me. And I'm exhilarated by the adventure of living to discover what those things are.

Since Jesus gave the Great Commission to all his disciples, it makes sense that all of us have some role to play in it. Whatever else God has "prepared in advance" for you, he almost certainly has called you to have a role in seeing his good news reach every people, every language, and every place. What might that role be?

Praying

Praying is one Great Commission task that everyone can do. Many can give; a few can go; but everyone can pray. Praying doesn't require a passport or financial resources—it merely requires a willing heart and discipline.

So if you are not already praying for the Great Commission, consider committing right now to do so. You can start with resources like Joshua Project's Unreached of the Day or join a focused campaign like 30 Days of Prayer for the Muslim World. You could sign up for International Prayer Council's 110 Cities initiative or for the prayer team of a favorite ministry. Email "prayer text" to info@ finishingfund.org to begin receiving daily prayer reminders about the unengaged.

Invite others to join you. Your church or small group could adopt a people group for prayer using materials from People-Groups.org or Operation World. You can use Prayercast videos to frame your intercession.

Praying may not seem like much of a contribution, but remember the Bible's promise that "the prayer of a righteous person is powerful and effective" (James 5:16). Your prayers, joined with those of millions of your brothers and sisters, have the power to conquer the kingdom of darkness and open doors to the gospel in every people group, every language, and every place. When we pray for the nations, we join Christ in his global mission—and help send the gospel where it has never gone before.

Giving

One thing Americans have that the Great Commission needs is money. According to the 2024 USA Wealth Report, Americans, who make up about 4 percent of the world's population, hold approximately 32 percent of the world's wealth—a staggering $67 trillion.[1] My friend Jim Wise of Blue Trust estimates at least $5 trillion of that is in the hands of committed believers.[2]

Many can give; a few can go; but everyone can pray.

How much will it cost to complete the Great Commission? We are already nearly done with the first goal, believers in every nation. Only a few million more dollars will be needed to get the work started in every people group. Illumi*Nations* estimates that the Bible in every language goal will require about a billion dollars—and a good part of that has already been raised.[3] The ACHIEVE Alliance says that planting a church in every place that does not yet have one might require $2 billion: possibly four million churches at a cost of about $500 per church.[4] So the total required to cross all three finish lines is probably no more than $3 billion. But even if the number is greater—say, $5 billion—it would represent only 0.1 percent of the wealth currently in the hands of committed American Christians. That's $1 out of every $1,000. In other words, we have more than enough resources—if we will release them.

Another problem, though, is misallocation. Remember from chapter 8 that only about 0.1 percent of everything Christians give is directed toward work among unreached people groups—again, about $1 dollar out of every $1,000 given. This highlights a critical need for redirecting our current giving toward unreached places. We don't just need to give generously, but we need to make sure that our gifts go to the right places.

That's all well and good, you might say, but I'm not wealthy. And in an American context, you may be right when you say that. But compared to the rest of the world, even ordinary Christians in the United States are extraordinarily rich. According to the Global Wealth Report, the *average* American adult ranks among the *top 10 percent* of the world's wealthiest individuals.[5] This means that many of us have more capacity than we think to make an impact on global missions through our giving.

Throughout this book, I've highlighted great ministries that are working at the front lines of the Great Commission, planting churches, translating the Bible, working among refugees, and so on. At the back of the book, you'll find a list of ministries and their websites that will take you directly to their home page. You can browse around to learn more, and if you like what you see, contribute online.

If you don't know which to choose, there are a handful of ministries that will, like a mutual fund, allocate your contributions toward high-impact Great Commission ministries and projects. One is Doulos Partners, which supports the efforts of several great church planting ministries. Their model ensures that 100 percent of donor funds go directly to the field.

Another is 500K, which is helping fuel church planting in India. Its name comes from the estimate that there are 500,000 (hence 500K) villages in India without churches.

For those with greater capacity, the Finishing Fund presents an opportunity to invest at the very frontier of the Great Commission. Finishing Fund donors commit at least $30,000 and then jointly fund projects that engage unengaged people groups and plant churches in places where there are none. In eight years, the partners of the Finishing Fund have helped engage 800 people groups with the gospel for the first time.

> Our generation is the first in history that is without excuse. Unlike our ancestors, we have everything we need to finish the task.

Another excellent option is IllumiNations, the collective alliance of Bible translation agencies and supporters committed to making Scripture available in every language by the year 2033. Like a mutual fund for translation, IllumiNations directs funding where the need and impact are greatest. Their unified approach is accelerating the work of translation.

Jim Wise says that our generation is the first in history that is without excuse. Unlike our ancestors, we have everything we need to finish the task. If we don't do it, it will be because we chose not to. The needed resources are already in our hands—the question is whether we will release them and properly direct them. And that is up to each of us.

Going

If praying and giving aren't enough for you, you can think about going. By going, I don't just mean sharing your faith with your friends, loved ones, and those God brings into your path. All of us have a responsibility to do that, and I hope you already are. What I mean by *going* is actively joining the effort to reach every people, every language, and every place with the gospel.

Going While Staying

In chapter 10 we talked about the Great Coming and saw how God has brought millions of people from the world's unreached places to America. It's a sure bet that some of them are living in your city. So the simplest and easiest way to go doesn't require much going at all. God has already brought these folks across the ocean and put them in your backyard. All you need to do to reach them is go across town.

Likely there are already people doing ministry among immigrants in your city. Seek them out, learn more about what they're doing, and ask them how you can help. Much of the work is just simple service: helping men find work, women learn to drive, kids with their schoolwork. As you serve, you will build relationships, and as you build relationships a time will come to share the gospel. Of course, you'll want to bathe all of that in prayer, asking God for connection and opportunity.

Who knows? Maybe you're the person God has chosen to lead an immigrant from Afghanistan or Syria to Christ. And maybe they will be the one to launch a movement of the gospel among their people or in their former place.

If you can't find a ministry already working with immigrants in your area, maybe God is calling you to start something. Contact Global Frontiers Missions or another of the ministries mentioned in chapter 10 and inquire about training opportunities. Talk to your pastor about whether your church might want to be involved. Then step out in faith to begin.

> Maybe you're the person God has chosen to lead an immigrant from Afghanistan or Syria to Christ.

Another similar opportunity is with international students. Is there a university in your town? Call the dean of students and ask how you can become a host for a student from another country, then invest in serving and loving some young person into the Kingdom. Or perhaps there is already a ministry serving international students in your city. Reach out to them and offer to help.

You might also consider volunteering with Global Media Outreach or another ministry using media or the Internet to reach the unreached. They need people to serve as online missionaries, responding to spiritual seekers from around the world through email, chat, and social media. They especially need multilingual volunteers who can help reach people in their heart languages. Just visit their website and look for the "Volunteer" button.

Going Overseas

But maybe God is calling you to go—to move overseas and become directly involved in the work in some distant place. If so, you should contact one or more of the ministries mentioned in this book to ask about their requirements and training programs for missionaries. They will help you assess your qualifications, pick a destination, and develop a plan for acquiring needed knowledge and skills, raising support, and building a prayer team.

THE WISE SERVANT

At the conclusion of Jesus' Olivet Discourse in Matthew 24, there are a series of parables that show us how we should live as we await Jesus' return. In the first, the Parable of the Wise Servant, Jesus exhorts his people to be hard at work, serving him and the church, right up until the end. He says, "Who then is the faithful and wise servant, whom the master has put in charge of the servants in his household to give them their food at the proper time? It will be good for that servant whose master finds him doing so when he returns. Truly I tell you, he will put him in charge of all his possessions" (vv. 45–47).

There are different ideas about what Jesus had in mind when he says, "Give them their food at the proper time." I think it describes meeting the needs of God's people and that "the faithful and wise servant" is any one of God's people—not just church leaders or pastors—who serves God by using his or her gifts to do so. As Peter says in 1 Peter 4:10, "Each of you should use whatever gift you have received to serve others, as faithful stewards of God's grace in its various forms." Paul makes the same point in Romans 12, where he urges us to use our gifts diligently for the benefit of our brothers and sisters—to prophesy, serve, teach, encourage, give, lead, and show mercy in accordance with the gifts we've received.

And notice the promise of reward: Jesus said, "It will be good for that servant whose master finds him doing so when he returns" and that he will put that servant "in charge of all his possessions." That's the same idea found in the Parable of the Talents: that those who are faithful in "investing" the gifts we've been given by God will be entrusted with greater responsibilities in his kingdom: "Well done, good and faithful servant. You have been faithful over a little; I will set you over much" (Matthew 25:21, ESV).

If Jesus is coming soon, now is the time to seize the opportunities he has given us.

In this same parable, Jesus contrasted the wise servant with another he calls "wicked." This servant represents a believer who squanders his gifts and his opportunity, abusing his "fellow servants" and living a worldly lifestyle, because he thinks his master will never return. Jesus said that when he comes, he will deal severely with such a servant, promising to "cut him to pieces and assign him a place with the hypocrites" (Matthew 24:48–51). Sobering.

Most of us are somewhere between these two extremes: We're not dissolute like the wicked servant, but we're also not pursuing the "good works, which God has prepared in advance for us to do" (Ephesians 2:10) as energetically as we might. Subconsciously, we believe that we'll have time later to get more involved in God's

Kingdom work. We're working hard in our jobs and raising our kids and don't feel we have the time and energy to devote to God's work. We're also easily sidetracked by the abundance of distractions that surround us.

But if Jesus is coming soon, now is the time to seize the opportunities he has given us. Are you using your gifts to the best of your ability to accomplish Jesus' Great Commission? Are you obeying Peter's command to "speed the coming" of that day?" If not, make today the day you reset your priorities and put your work for God's Kingdom at the top of your list. Our generation has an opportunity unlike any that has come before: By God's grace, we can be the ones to finish the task. Don't miss your chance to be part of the great sprint to the finish.

PART FOUR

The Celebration

CHAPTER 14

The Celebration

Have you ever seen film of VJ Day? After many long years of war, Japan's surrender brought tremendous joy to the world. Huge crowds gathered in the streets of London, New York, and many other cities. Old and young, people cheered, laughed, sang, danced, and embraced, expressing their elation that peace had finally come. It was a remarkable celebration of a victory hard won.

But all of that is nothing compared to the celebration that will follow the completion of the Great Commission. Matthew 24:14 promises that finishing the Great Commission race will bring about the end of the age and the return of Christ: "This gospel of the kingdom will be preached in the whole world as a testimony to all nations, and then the end will come." And for God's people, that will be a celebration such as the world has never seen. We'll enthusiastically praise God's incredible victory in bringing his kingdom to every people, language, and place. And we'll begin an eternal journey of blessing so wonderful it can scarcely be conceived.

So let's look ahead to that celebration and consider what Jesus' return will bring about for those who love him.

WHEN WILL IT BE?

First, remember that the Bible teaches that no one can know exactly when that day will come. It gives us hints and clues that help us know that the end is near but warns against trying to pick an hour or a day—or even a year, in my opinion.

> The celebration that will accompany the completion of the Great Commission will be like nothing the world has ever seen.

Nevertheless, Matthew 24:14 does link Jesus' return and the end of the age with the completion of the Great Commission. And in Romans 11, where Paul talks about God's plan for Israel, he says that "Israel has experienced a hardening in part until the full number of the Gentiles has come in" (Romans 11:25). Again, this links the completion of the Great Commission to the events of the end times, when God will soften the hearts of Israel through the Great Tribulation and ultimately bring many of them to salvation.

In fairness, we can't be sure exactly where the Great Commission finish lines lie. Peter tells us that "the Lord . . . is patient . . . not wanting anyone to perish, but everyone to come to repentance" (2 Peter 3:9). Even after the gospel has been preached to every people group, in every language, and in every place, Jesus may tarry so that every possible person has the chance to hear.

But once we've crossed those three finish lines, the door will be open for the return of Christ. We can't know for certain if he will return immediately, but based on Jesus' promise, the clock will be ticking, and he could come at any time. I think it will be soon.

THE RAPTURE

I believe the first event in the return of Christ will be the rapture, when God's people from around the world are gathered to him. The primary teaching about the rapture is found in 1 Thessalonians 4:16–18, which says,

> For the Lord himself will come down from heaven, with a loud command, with the voice of the archangel and with the trumpet call of God, and the dead in Christ will rise first. After that, we who are still alive and are left will be caught up together with them in the clouds to meet the Lord in the air. And so we will be with the Lord forever. Therefore encourage one another with these words.

The Greek word translated "caught up" is *harpazo*, which means to seize, catch up, snatch away, or carry off. The Vulgate Bible used the Latin word *rapio* to translate *harpazo*, which is where we get the English term *rapture*. The idea is that Jesus will return without setting foot on the earth; that he will issue "a loud command"; that the dead in Christ will be resurrected; that they, along with all believers who are alive at that time, will be "gathered to him" in the air; and that he will take us from there to heaven.

There is disagreement about the timing of the rapture, but I believe it will take place before the beginning of the Great

Tribulation. During the Tribulation, God's wrath will be poured out on the unbelieving world in judgment for sin. I believe the church will not be present for that judgment because "we have not been appoint[ed] to suffer wrath" (1 Thessalonians 5:9).

TRANSFORMED

Just before we are raptured, Paul teaches in 1 Corinthians 15:51–52 that we will be transformed: "Listen, I tell you a mystery: We will not all sleep, *but we will all be changed*—in a flash, in the twinkling of an eye, at the last trumpet. For the trumpet will sound, the dead will be raised imperishable, and we will be changed."

When that last trumpet blows, the dead in Christ will be raised in new, "imperishable" bodies, and the bodies of those who are alive will be instantly transformed.

What will these new bodies be like? Paul gives us a hint in Philippians 3:21, when he says that on that day Jesus "will transform our lowly bodies *so that they will be like his glorious body*." Likewise, in 1 Corinthians 15:42–44 he says, "The body that is sown is perishable, it is raised imperishable; it is sown in dishonor, it is raised in glory; it is sown in weakness, it is raised in power; it is sown a natural body, it is raised a spiritual body."

The Bible promises that all believers will receive new glorified resurrection bodies.

It's difficult to know exactly what these descriptions mean. What is a "spiritual body" after all? But from what we can understand, we know that these new bodies are going to be amazing:

Imperishable, no longer subject to death and decay

Glorified, with no "sin nature" or "flesh"—*sarx* in the Greek

Powerful, with superhuman abilities like those Jesus had in his resurrection body

In the common view of heaven, we exist eternally as spirits without physical bodies, floating among the clouds, with halos, playing harps. There is literally nothing correct about that image. The Bible makes clear that we will have real, physical bodies for eternity. We'll have faces and names. We'll eat and drink, worship, work, and (probably) play in our glorified bodies. What's more, we will not float among the clouds but will return to the earth—a New Earth—where we'll live forever. And we won't while away the eons plucking on harps; we will have meaningful, stimulating work to do for God forever and ever.

REUNION

One of the great blessings of eternity will be our reunion with believing loved ones who have preceded us in death. They will be raised, and their bodies will be transformed along with ours. We'll experience joyful reunions with family members and friends from whom we have been separated—reunions that will include smiles, hugs, and kisses, thanks to our new bodies—and we'll enjoy intimate relationships with them for eternity.

We'll also experience "reunion" with people we've never met but with whom we share important connections. If you've supported Great Commission work, you have a connection with the people who were brought to Christ through those efforts. Even

> One of the great blessings of eternity will be our reunion with believing loved ones who have preceded us in death.

though you've never met them and couldn't communicate with them today if you did, you'll have the joy of meeting them, exploring your kingdom connection, and praising Jesus together for his goodness in your lives. I can't wait to meet some of my new friends!

THE WEDDING SUPPER

One of the metaphors the Bible uses to describe the church is "the bride of Christ," and there are interesting parallels between our relationship with Jesus and the wedding customs of first-century Jews.

For one thing, weddings in those days were celebrated with a great feast that might continue for up to seven days. And Revelation 19:9 promises a great wedding feast to celebrate the union of Christ and his church. The wedding supper will mark the beginning of a new, eternal, intimate phase of our union with Jesus. Amazingly, Luke 12:37 says that Jesus will "dress himself to serve" and will "come and wait on" us as we "recline at the table."

By now you understand that the church—the bride—will include men and women from every one of the world's people groups, languages, and places. If you've traveled much, you know that people from different places enjoy a wide variety of foods. I love steak and potatoes, but my Nigerian friend Daniel likes nothing better than his pounded yam and egusi soup. Can you imagine the diversity of the delicacies at the Wedding Feast, where our bridegroom, who desires to please his bride, offers each of us the foods we relish?

REWARDS

The Bible teaches that God has saved us to do good works and prepared those works for us to do (Ephesians 2:10). He has also equipped us for them by giving us spiritual gifts (Romans 12; 1 Corinthians 12). And if all of that wasn't enough, God has also promised to reward us for work we do in his name. Matthew 16:27 says, "For the Son of Man is going to come in his Father's glory with his angels, and then *he will reward each person* according to what they have done."

Christ will judge our works and grant our rewards sometime during the seven-year period between the rapture and the return of Christ, at what is called the *bema* judgment. Paul writes about this in 2 Corinthians 5:10: "For we must all appear before the judgment seat [*bema*] of Christ, so that each of us may receive what is due us for the things done while in the body, whether good or bad."

At the *bema*, everything we've done as believers will be tested with fire (1 Corinthians 3:13–15). Some things—good works Paul compares to "gold, silver, and precious stones"—will survive and result in rewards. Others—works of "wood, hay, and straw"—will burn up. There will be no rewards for such acts.

As Paul makes clear, this judgment has nothing to do with our salvation. Even if everything a person brings burns at the *bema*, that person "will be saved." They will enter eternity without rewards, but will nevertheless enjoy eternity with Jesus and with God. Our salvation does not depend on the quality of our works: We are not saved by anything we do but by faith in Jesus Christ.

It's hard to say exactly what form these promised rewards will take. The Scriptures speak of crowns (1 Corinthians 9), garments (Revelation 19), and treasure in heaven (1 Timothy 6). From the parable of the ten minas, it seems that one form of reward will be increased authority and responsibility in the millennial kingdom and perhaps even into eternity (Luke 19:17). The idea is that our faithfulness in this life qualifies us for higher degrees of responsibility in the kingdom.

> God has promised to reward us for the work we do in his name.

I hope the idea of eternal rewards fills you with anticipation and joy. But if you're wondering whether you've accomplished anything for Jesus that will survive at the *bema*, now is the time to get to work. How has God equipped you to join the sprint to the finish? What has the Spirit gifted you to do? What opportunities has God put in your path? Begin exercising those gifts and seizing those opportunities. You'll enjoy the fruits of that labor for a long time.[1]

TRIBULATION

While we are with Jesus in paradise, celebrating our marriage to him and receiving our rewards, God will be pouring out judgment on the earth. Those terrible times are prophesied in Daniel 12:1 and Revelation 6 through 19. Jesus himself spoke of them in Matthew 24:21–22.

Interestingly, there will be a continuation of the Great Commission during the Tribulation. Revelation 14:6 speaks of an angelic messenger who "had the eternal gospel to proclaim to those who live on the earth—to every nation, tribe, language and people." This angel represents the final piece of God's Great Tribulation evangelical push that includes the two witnesses in Revelation 11 and the 144,000 missionaries in Revelation 13.

The implication of this verse is that every person who is alive in those days will hear the good news through this supernatural messenger. I see this as one final expression of God's incredible grace and mercy toward a rebellious world, and a vindication of his justice. Thanks to this divine messenger, no one alive in those days will be able to argue that they did not know about God's amazing love for humankind and his incredible provision for our sin.

It is important to note, though, that none of this is accomplished by the church, which will no longer exist in its present form on the earth. God himself will do this work.

THE MILLENNIUM

At the end of that seven-year tribulation, the church will return with Jesus to the earth. There will be a great battle—Armageddon—between the forces of the world, under the leadership of the antichrist, and Jesus Christ and "the armies of heaven . . ." This battle will be a rout—the world's army will be destroyed, and its leaders, the beast (that's the antichrist), and his false prophet will be captured and cast into the "fiery lake of burning sulfur" forever.

Following his victory at Armageddon, Jesus will assume the throne of his ancestor David and begin to rule over the earth from

Jerusalem. Zechariah 14:9 promises, "The LORD will be king over the whole earth. On that day there will be one LORD, and his name the only name."

According to Revelation 20:6, this period of Christ's rule on this earth will last for one thousand years. During this time we—the church—"will be priests of God and of Christ and will reign with him."

The Bible has a lot to say about this thousand-year reign of Christ, commonly called the *millennium*. During this period, the earth will be populated by those who survived the tribulation and by their descendants, who will enjoy supernaturally long lifespans (Isaiah 65:20). The millennium will also bring unmatched prosperity to the earth (Amos 9:13). According to Revelation 20:3, Satan will be bound in "the Abyss" and constrained from "deceiving the nations anymore until the thousand years were ended." Satan's absence will help make the millennium a time of righteousness, godliness, peace, and justice.

At the end of the millennium, Satan "will be released from his prison and will go out to deceive the nations" (Revelation 20:7–8), stirring them up into rebellion against Jesus. But this rebellion will be quickly overcome, and Satan will be "thrown into the lake of burning sulfur" where he "will be tormented day and night for ever and ever" (Revelation 20:9–10). At last, after that final battle, our enemy, Satan, will be done away with once and for all.

THE NEW HEAVEN AND EARTH

Finally, after all of that, God promises that he will re-create the universe. Revelation 21:1 says, "Then I saw 'a new heaven and a new earth,' for the first heaven and the first earth had passed away." We can only guess what this new creation will be like. Will the same laws of physics apply? Will there be new kinds of plants and animals? Will the new heavens have stars, planets, and galaxies?

God will also reveal a beautiful city—the New Jerusalem—where we will live with him forever. According to Revelation 21, this new city will be immense and spectacular, built of and decorated with every kind of precious stone. I think it is this New Jerusalem that Jesus was talking about when he told his disciples he was going "to prepare a place for" them (John 14:2). Jesus, the Divine Carpenter, has been working for nearly 2,000 years to build this new city, which will be our home for eternity. It's going to be something.

> *In the beginning, God walked with Adam in the Garden. In the end, he will walk with us in the city.*

In Revelation 21:3–5, John describes for us what life will be like in this new creation:

> *God will live with us.* In the beginning, God walked with Adam in the garden. In the end, he will live with us in the city. When it's all said and done, we don't go to live with him in heaven; he comes to live with us on the new earth. We will see him face to face and enjoy his personal presence forever. We'll be "his people" and he will be "our God"—a degree of intimacy and familiarity we cannot conceive today.

He will wipe away every tear. All of us will experience sadness on the eve of eternity. We'll regret sins we committed or opportunities and rewards we squandered. We'll mourn loved ones who are not with us. But God promises to comfort us personally, wiping away every tear. And from that point on, there will be no more crying or pain—only the joy of being in continual relationship with our Maker and Redeemer.

Death will be a memory. We'll never again experience death or decay. There won't even be pain! According to Revelation 20, death itself will be destroyed and "thrown into the lake of fire." At last, our enemy, death, will be destroyed.

Everything will be new! When the story of this creation has come to an end, God will create an entirely new reality for his people. We'll enjoy exploring and learning about this new creation forever and ever.

John goes on to tell us that the New Jerusalem—our eternal home—will not have a temple because "the Lord God Almighty and the Lamb are its temple" (Revelation 21:22). In other words, God and Jesus will live openly in the city, not confined to some sacred building. The city will not need the sun or the moon for light, because "the glory of God gives it light, and the Lamb is its lamp" (v. 23). Its gates will never "be shut," signaling that it will exist forever in perfect peace and safety (v. 25). There will be a "river of the water of life, as clear as crystal, flowing from the throne of God and of the Lamb down the middle of the great street of the city," and along the river will be "the tree of life" (Revelation 22:1–2). The New Jerusalem will be a place of abundant, overflowing life.

Revelation 22 also teaches that we will serve God forever. In other words, we'll work. But it promises that "no longer will there be any curse" (v. 3), so our work will be vastly different from anything we've ever experienced. Instead of endless toil just to outpace the decay, our work will be fruitful and the things we create will endure. Part of our work will be to "reign for ever and ever" (v. 5) with him and his Son over the new creation he has made for us.

HE'S COMING SOON

We don't have long to wait. I've made the case in this book that the Great Commission is nearing completion and that its completion will open the door for Jesus' return. And that's not the only clue we're living in the very last days. Israel has been regathered now for nearly a generation. We're at the end of 6,000 years of biblical history, and we're coming up on the 2,000-year anniversary of the resurrection. As prophesied, people are traveling like never before, knowledge is exploding, our culture is in decline, and the church in the West is experiencing increasing persecution and apostasy.[2]

Let's each do our part to "hasten the coming of that day" by joining the sprint to the finish of the Great Commission.

In other words, Jesus is coming soon. Before long, the final trumpet is going to sound, the dead in Christ will be raised, those of us who are still alive will be transformed, and we'll all be gathered to "meet the Lord in the air." That will begin the sequence of events described in this chapter.

Let's look forward with joy and exhilaration to the coming of that day and all the incredible blessings that will follow it. But more than that, let's each do our part to "hasten the coming of that day" by joining the sprint to the finish of the Great Commission. By God's grace, we won't have to run much longer, because the finish line is in sight. And when we cross it, the celebration will begin.

Maranatha. Come soon, Lord Jesus.

APPENDIX 1

How Many People Groups Remain?

At the time of this writing, PeopleGroups.org says that there are about 3,200 remaining unengaged groups. Yet in chapter 6 I say that the number is under 100. That's an enormous difference—how can it be explained? Well, as I said in chapter 6, the answers you get when counting people groups depend a lot on the assumptions you make. And FTT/The Finishing Fund and PeopleGroups.org make different assumptions that result in significantly different answers.

For one thing, PeopleGroups.org considers almost 500 people groups with non-evangelical Christian heritage—Orthodox, Catholic, Coptic, even Anglican—to be unengaged. I understand why they make that choice, but to my mind there is a big difference between a Hindu group in India where the name of Jesus has never been proclaimed and a majority-Catholic group in Europe where he is worshipped weekly.

In addition, PeopleGroups.org includes nearly 900 listings of the diaspora populations of people groups. The Japanese, for instance, are listed nine times—in Argentina, Bolivia, China, the Dominican Republic, France, Germany, Micronesia, Portugal, and Taiwan—even though they are *not* unengaged in Japan. These diaspora populations are surely worthy of evangelism, but in my judgment getting to these diaspora populations is not as urgent as reaching groups where no one has ever heard.

PeopleGroups.org also includes nearly 100 deaf groups. The deaf are a special case when thinking about people groups, and while I agree that we need to work to see movements among the deaf in every place, because of the differences between the deaf and other groups, at the Finishing Fund we list them separately.

But by far the biggest factor is that the PeopleGroups.org list includes many hundreds of groups that have been engaged successfully by other ministries. One example is the Hanne people of Ethiopia and Somalia. I have been there myself and heard the amazing stories of how the gospel broke into their world. Another is the Yardima people of Nepal, where a church has been meeting on the grounds of the Hindu temple for more than five years. PeopleGroups.org chooses not to report these groups as engaged until an IMB representative has verified that there is a movement of the gospel among them.

When these differences and others like them are reconciled, the discrepancy between the two lists largely disappears.

APPENDIX 2

Must the Church Complete the Great Commission?

Throughout this book, I've made the case that Jesus will not return until the Great Commission has been completed—until there are disciples in every people group and the good news has been preached in every place. As Jesus said, in Matthew 24:14, "This gospel of the kingdom will be preached in the whole world as a testimony to all nations, *and then the end will come.*"

But is it necessary for the church to complete the Great Commission before the rapture? Or is it possible that the task will be completed by God after the rapture, during the Great Tribulation? In this appendix I want to consider the biblical evidence for both points of view and explain why I think it is the church's responsibility to finish the task before we are taken up by our Lord.

Those who feel that the Great Commission will be finished after the rapture point to the amazing evangelistic work that God has promised to accomplish during the tribulation. First, Revelation

11 tells us about the two witnesses who will prophesy from Jerusalem for the first three and a half years of the tribulation. Thanks to modern technology, the testimony of the witnesses will be available everywhere on the planet. When they are finally killed, we're told, "some from every people, tribe, language and nation will gaze upon their bodies" (Revelation 11:9).

In addition, Revelation 7 speaks of the 144,000 Jewish servants of God. Many think that these servants will travel the world during the tribulation preaching the good news.

And if that wasn't enough, Revelation 14:6 tells us that God will dispatch an angelic evangelist who will proclaim the good news to every person on the planet: "Then I saw another angel flying in midair, and he had the eternal gospel to proclaim to those who live on the earth—to every nation, tribe, language and people."

So there is no doubt that the good news will be preached "in the whole world, as a testimony to all nations" during the great tribulation. And since the church will have been raptured before these things take place, we will not have a role in that work.

But does that relieve the church of the responsibility to "go and make disciples of all nations" (Matthew 28:19)? I don't think so. First, Jesus gave this command to the apostles and, through them, to the church. It is evident from the way they responded that they took that command seriously. What's more, I think Jesus expected them to complete it. It's possible that this command was aspirational—like the instruction to "be perfect, as your Father in heaven is perfect"—but my conviction is that Jesus meant what he said: that he wants us to be the ones to "make disciples of all nations."

That conviction is strengthened by the fact that we are so close to completing the work. Generations of faithful believers have labored to take the gospel to "the whole world" with no hope of seeing it finished. Today, though, we're within a few years of seeing it accomplished, and the gospel is spreading like wildfire in places where Jesus's name has never been heard. I think that, by God's grace, we'll be able to start in all the rest of the world's *ethnos* within the next year or two. And the every language and every place finish lines are not far behind. Surely he isn't going to come for us just before we complete the race.

What's more, Revelation 7 describes a great crowd from "every nation, tribe, people and language" surrounding the throne of the Lamb. The angel tells John that "these are those who have come out of the great tribulation." Many think that this crowd is made up of tribulation martyrs—that "taken out of" describes their death during the tribulation. But the phrase describes at least as well those who are "taken out" of the world before the beginning of the tribulation—in other words, the raptured church, comprised of people from every *ethnos*. Certainly the description of that crowd as being "a great multitude that no one could count" seems to fit better the entire church than the relatively smaller number who will be martyred in the tribulation.

And isn't it necessary that God's church include people from every *ethnos*? Ephesians 2 describes the process by which Christ is reversing Babel, reuniting the nations God separated there into "one new man"—his body, the church—and "in that one body" reconciling "them to God through the cross." Is it possible that

God will rapture his church *before* that process is completed and the body of Christ is whole? I can't imagine it.

It's important to understand exactly what the Great Commission requires of the church: not that we preach the gospel to every person but that we make disciples "of all nations." I think it is likely that not every person will hear the gospel before the rapture—although we're getting closer to that goal as well—and that God, in his incredible grace, will complete that task after the church has been raptured. At the same time, though, I believe that Christ will not come for his church until we have completed the task he gave us: to take the good news to every nation, every language, and every place.

But what about the doctrine of imminence, which says that the rapture could take place at any time? This doctrine is based on numerous biblical passages about the unpredictability of Jesus's return, such as Matthew 24:36 ("About that day or hour no one knows, not even the angels in heaven, nor the Son, but only the Father.") and Matthew 24:42 ("Therefore keep watch, because you do not know on what day your Lord will come"). Imminence teaches that there is nothing that must occur before the rapture takes place—that there are no preconditions to it. So how can I argue that the rapture must wait until after the Great Commission has been completed?

My answer would be that while the Bible does say that Christ "will come at an hour when you do not expect him" (Matthew 24:44) and warns us to be ready for his return at any time, it also describes several things that apparently must take place before the rapture. For example, was it possible for the rapture to occur and the church be removed from the world before Israel was regathered? I can't imagine how, unless the period between the rapture and the beginning of the Great Tribulation was decades or centuries long—something I don't think the prophecy of the seventy weeks in Daniel 9 permits.

To go back even further, would it have been possible for the rapture to take place before the destruction of Jerusalem in 70 AD? Or is it possible that the rapture could happen before the prophecies of apostasy in the church in the last days (Matthew 24:10–12 and others) have been realized? (This one seems particularly problematic—after all, how could the church apostatize after it has been raptured?) These and other biblical clues suggest that while the rapture may be "imminent" today, until recently it was not. I see the completion of the Great Commission as another thing the Bible says must take place before the rapture occurs.

Fortunately, we don't have long to wait. By God's grace, very soon there will be disciples in all the world's *ethne*, the Bible in every language, and a church in every place, and for the first time in history, the door will open for the return of Christ. May it be soon! Maranatha! Come quickly, Lord Jesus!

ENDNOTES

Introduction

1. "51% of Churchgoers Don't Know of the Great Commission," Barna, March 27, 2018, https://www.barna.com/research/half-churchgoers-not-heard-great-commission/

Chapter 1

1. I've changed the name of this people group and the others mentioned in this book for their protection
2. There are fewer languages than people groups because many people groups share languages.
3. Steven Hawthorne, *Perspectives on the World Christian Movement: The Study Guide,* 2009 Edition (William Carey Publishing, 2009), 4.

Chapter 5

1. Rodney Stark, *The Rise of Christianity* (HarperSanFrancisco, 1996), 74–75.
2. Kenneth Scott Latourette, *A History of Christianity*, vol. 1 (Harper & Brothers, 1953), 162–63.
3. Peter Brown, *The World of Late Antiquity* (Harcourt Brace Jovanovich, 1971), 82–83.

ENDNOTES

4. Henry Chadwick, *The Early Church* (Penguin Books, 1967), 231.
5. Thomas Cahill, *How the Irish Saved Civilization* (Nan A. Talese, 1995), 101–3.
6. Anders Winroth, *The Conversion of Scandinavia* (Yale University Press, 2012), 134–36.
7. Latourette, *A History of Christianity*, 1:245.
8. Latourette, *A History of Christianity*, 1:360–61.
9. Einhard, *Life of Charlemagne*, trans. Lewis Thorpe (Penguin Books, 1969), chap. 7.
10. Richard Fletcher, *The Barbarian Conversion: From Paganism to Christianity* (Henry Holt, 1997), 235.
11. Latourette, *A History of Christianity*, 1:413–14.
12. Jonathan Riley-Smith, *The Crusades: A History*, 2nd ed. (Yale University Press, 2005), 298.
13. C. H. Lawrence, *The Friars: The Impact of the Early Mendicant Movement on Western Society* (Longman, 1994), 89–90.
14. John H. Elliott, *Empires of the Atlantic World* (Yale University Press, 2006), 67.
15. Bartolomé de las Casas, *A Short Account of the Destruction of the Indies*, trans. Nigel Griffin (Penguin Books, 1992), 12.
16. Andrew Walls, *The Missionary Movement in Christian History* (Orbis Books, 1996), 104–5.
17. John W. O'Malley, *The First Jesuits* (Harvard University Press, 1993), 278.
18. Walls, *Missionary Movement*, 112–13.
19. John Thornton, *Africa and Africans in the Making of the Atlantic World, 1400–1800* (Cambridge University Press, 1992), 192.
20. Walls, *Missionary Movement*, 85.
21. Mark A. Noll, *The New Shape of World Christianity* (IVP Academic, 2009), 34.
22. Walls, *Missionary Movement*, 79–80.
23. Colin Podmore, *The Moravian Church in England*, 1728–1760 (Clarendon Press, 1998), 56.

24. John Wesley, Journal, May 24, 1738.

25. Walls, *Missionary Movement*, 81–82.

26. Kenneth Scott Latourette, *A History of the Expansion of Christianity*, vol. 4 (Harper & Brothers, 1941), 1.

27. William Carey, *An Enquiry into the Obligations of Christians* (Leicester, 1792), 7.

28. Robert Morrison, *Memoirs of the Life and Labours of Robert Morrison* (Longman, Orme, Brown, Green, and Longmans, 1839), 45.

29. Walls, *Missionary Movement*, 103-5.

30. Hudson Taylor, *A Retrospect* (China Inland Mission, 1894), 23.

31. Dana L. Robert, *American Women in Mission* (Mercer University Press, 1996), 62.

32. Courtney Anderson, *To the Golden Shore: The Life of Adoniram Judson* (Little, Brown, 1956), 321.

33. John R. Mott, *The Evangelization of the World in This Generation* (Student Volunteer Movement for Foreign Missions, 1900), 15.

34. Patricia R. Hill, *The World Their Household* (University of Michigan Press, 1985), 103.

35. David Livingstone, *Missionary Travels and Researches in South Africa* (John Murray, 1857), 8.

36. Andrew Walls, *The Missionary Movement in Christian History* (1996), 144–145.

37. Brian Stanley, *The World Missionary Conference, Edinburgh 1910* (Grand Rapids: Eerdmans, 2009), 3.

38. Allan Anderson, *An Introduction to Pentecostalism: Global Charismatic Christianity* (Cambridge University Press, 2004), 45.

39. David Aikman, *Jesus in Beijing: How Christianity Is Transforming China and Changing the Global Balance of Power* (Regnery Publishing, 2003).

40. Loren Cunningham, *Is That Really You, God?: Hearing the Voice of God* (YWAM Publishing, 1984).

41. Billy Graham, *The Lausanne Covenant* (Lausanne Committee for World Evangelization, 1974), Introduction.

42. Billy Graham Evangelistic Association, *Amsterdam 2000: A Global Celebration of Evangelists* (Billy Graham Evangelistic Association, 2000).

Chapter 6

1. Ralph D. Winter, "The New Macedonia: A Revolutionary New Era in Mission Begins," in *Perspectives on the World Christian Movement: A Reader*, 4th ed., ed. Ralph D. Winter, Steven C. Hawthorne (William Carey Library, 2009), 347

2. Yvonne Wood Hunneycutt, "New Pioneers Leading the Way in the Final Era" in *Perspectives on the World Christian Movement: A Reader*, 4th ed., ed. Ralph D. Winter, Steven C. Hawthorne (William Carey Library, 2009), 379

3. Hunneycutt, "New Pioneers Leading the Way in the Final Era," 379–80.

4. Joshua Project, "Global Dashboard," Joshua Project, accessed April 2, 2025, https://joshuaproject.net/people_groups/dashboard.

5. International Mission Board, "People Groups Official Web Site," PeopleGroups.org, accessed April 2, 2025, https://peoplegroups.org.

6. Joshua Project, "Turk in Türkiye (Turkey)," Joshua Project, accessed June 4, 2025, https://joshuaproject.net/people_groups/18274/TU.

7. International Mission Board, "People Groups Official Web Site."

Chapter 7

1. Bruce M. Metzger, *The Early Versions of the New Testament: Their Origin, Transmission, and Limitations* (Clarendon Press, 1977), 3–5.

2. Metzger, *Early Versions of the New Testament*, 28-38.

3. David Daniell, *The Bible in English: Its History and Influence* (Yale University Press, 2003), 66–68.

4. Martin Luther, *Preface to the New Testament*, trans. Charles M. Jacobs, in *Works of Martin Luther*, vol. 6 (Muhlenberg Press, 1960).

5. David Daniell, *William Tyndale: A Biography* (Yale University Press, 1994), 128-40, 379-82.

6. Kenneth Scott Latourette, *A History of Christianity*, vol. 2 (Harper & Brothers, 1953), 789.

7. Alister McGrath, *In the Beginning: The Story of the King James Bible and How It Changed a Nation, a Language, and a Culture* (Anchor Books, 2001), 203.

8. Latourette, *A History of Christianity*, 2:1002.

9. Courtney Anderson, *To the Golden Shore: The Life of Adoniram Judson* (Little, Brown, 1956), 321–323.

10. George Smith, *The Life of William Carey* (John Murray, 1885), 156.

11. Wycliffe Global Alliance, "Scripture Access Statistics, 1900 estimate, updated 2020", https://www.wycliffe.net/resources/statistics/.

12. William A. Smalley, *Translation as Mission: Bible Translation in the Modern Missionary Movement* (Mercer University Press, 1991), 45–47.

13. Seed Company, *Annual Report 2024* (Seed Company, 2024), 3.

14. Deaf Bible Society, "ASL Bible Completion Announcement," 2020, https://www.deafbiblesociety.com/blog/asl-bible-complete.

15. Wycliffe Global Alliance, *Sign Language Translation Progress Report* (2024), 2, https://www.wycliffe.net.

16. unfoldingWord, *Open Bible Stories* (2024), 2, https://unfoldingword.org/obs.

17. illumiNations, *2024 Impact Report* (April 2024), 6, https://illuminations.bible.

18. *Ethnologue: Languages of the World*, 28th ed. (SIL International, 2025), 12–14.

19. Wycliffe Global Alliance, "Scripture Access Statistics," September 2024, 1–2, https://www.wycliffe.net.

20. illumiNations, *All-Access Goals* (2023), 1, https://illuminations.bible.

21. Todd Peterson, text message to the author, September 1, 2025.

ENDNOTES

Chapter 8

1. Joshua Project, "Malay in Malaysia," accessed April 3, 2025, https://joshuaproject.net/people_groups/13437/MY.
2. George Patterson, "The Spontaneous Multiplication of Churches," in *Perspectives on the World Christian Movement: A Reader*, ed. Ralph D. Winter and Steven C. Hawthorne, 4th ed. (William Carey Library, 2009), 602–10.
3. Roland Allen, *The Spontaneous Expansion of the Church and the Causes Which Hinder It* (Eerdmans, 1962).
4. George Patterson, *Obedience Oriented Education* (William Carey Library, 1976).
5. Curtis Sergeant, Zúme Training Guidebook (Midlothian, VA: WIGTake Resources, 2017), 5–10, https://zume.training/downloads/zume_guidebook.pdf.
6. To learn more about disciple-making movements, I recommend Jerry Trousdale, *Miraculous Movements: How Hundreds of Thousands of Muslims Are Falling in Love with Jesus* (Thomas Nelson, 2012); David L. Watson and Paul D. Watson, *Contagious Disciple Making: Leading Others on a Journey of Discovery* (Thomas Nelson, 2014); and Steve Smith with Ying Kai, T4T: *A Discipleship Re-Revolution* (WIGTake Resources, 2011). These books offer deep insights into DMM's emphasis on Discovery Bible Studies, organic disciple multiplication, and transformative growth in challenging contexts.
7. Nathan and Kari Shank, "Four Fields of Kingdom Growth," *International Journal of Frontier Missiology* 28, no. 1 (2011).
8. Steve Smith with Ying Kai, T4T: A Discipleship Re-Revolution (WIGTake Resources, 2011), 145–147.
9. To learn more about church planting movements, I recommend David Garrison, *Church Planting Movements: How God Is Redeeming a Lost World* (WIGTake Resources, 2004); Steve Smith with Ying Kai, *T4T: A Discipleship Re-Revolution* (WIGTake Resources,

2011); and George Patterson and Richard Scoggins, *Church Multiplication Guide: The Miracle of Church Reproduction*, rev. ed. (William Carey Library, 2002).

10. 24:14 Coalition, "Movement Basics," accessed April 3, 2025, https://2414now.net/movement-basics/.
11. Personal Interview by Doug Lucas with Bill Smith at 10am on Oct. 10, 2018, at Twelve House Training Center, 12 Chestnut Road, London.
12. 24:14 Coalition, "Resources," accessed April 3, 2025, https://2414 now.net/resources/#global-movement-statistics.
13. GACx (Global Alliance for Church Multiplication), "About," accessed April 3, 2025, https://gacx.io/about.
14. Dan Hitzhusen, interview by author, February 23, 2025. For more on the Bhojpuri Movement, see Victor John with Dave Coles, *Bhojpuri Breakthrough: A Movement That Keeps Multiplying* (WIGTake Resources, 2019.
15. The Traveling Team, "Money and Missions," accessed April 3, 2025, https://www.thetravelingteam.org/money-and-missions/.
16. Ralph D. Winter and Bruce A. Koch, "Finishing the Task: The Unreached Peoples Challenge" in *Perspectives on the World Christian Movement: A Reader*, 4th ed., ed. Ralph D. Winter, Steven C. Hawthorne (William Carey Library, 2009), 543
17. Statista Research Department, "Total Population of Sub-Saharan Africa from 1950 to 2023," Statista, January 2024, https://www.statista.com/statistics/805605/total-population-sub-saharan-africa/; "World Population," Wikipedia, last modified April 11, 2025, https://en.wikipedia.org/wiki/World_population; United Nations, "Population," United Nations, accessed April 11, 2025, https://www.un.org/en/global-issues/population.
18. Leslie T. Lyall, *A Passion for the Impossible: The Continuing Story of the Mission Hudson Taylor Began* (OMF Books, 1965), 5.

Chapter 9

1. Steven Hawthorne, *Perspectives on the World Christian Movement: The Study Guide,* 2009 Edition (William Carey Publishing, 2009), 61.

2. United Nations Department of Economic and Social Affairs, Population Division, *International Migrant Stock 2024: Key Facts and Figures,* accessed April 3, 2025, https://www.un.org/development/desa /pd/sites/www.un.org.development.desa.pd/files/undesa_pd_2025 _intlmigstock_2024_key_facts_and_figures_advance-unedited.pdf

3. International Organization for Migration, *World Migration Report 2024,* accessed April 3, 2025, https://worldmigrationreport.iom .int/msite/wmr-2024-interactive/.

4. United Nations High Commissioner for Refugees (UNHCR), "Over One Million Sea Arrivals Reach Europe in 2015," December 30, 2015, https://www.unhcr.org/news/stories/over-one-million -sea-arrivals-reach-europe-2015.

5. U.S. Department of Homeland Security, Office of Homeland Security Statistics, "U.S. Lawful Permanent Residents: 2023," September 2024, https://ohss.dhs.gov/sites/default/files/2024-09/2024 _0906_plcy_lawful_permanent_residents_fy2023.pdf.

6. U.S. Department of Homeland Security, Office of Homeland Security Statistics, "Estimates of the Unauthorized Immigrant Population Residing in the United States: January 2018–January 2022," June 2024, https://ohss.dhs.gov/sites/default/files/2024-06 /2024_0418_ohss_estimates-of-the-unauthorized-immigrant -population-residing-in-the-united-states-january-2018–january -2022.pdf.

7. Institute of International Education, *Open Doors 2024 Report on International Educational Exchange* (IIE, 2024), 12–14, 24–25, https://opendoorsdata.org/annual-release/.

8. United Nations, Department of Economic and Social Affairs, Population Division, *World Urbanization Prospects: The 2024 Revi-*

sion (United Nations, 2024), 1–2, https://population.un.org/wup /Publications/Files/WUP2024-Highlights.pdf.

9. Max Bearak, Dylan Moriarty, and Júlia Ledur, "How Africa Will Become the Center of the World's Urban Future," *The Washington Post*, November 19, 2021, https://www.washingtonpost.com/world /interactive/2021/africa-cities/.

Chapter 10

1. The JESUS Film Project, email message to author, "New Languages Milestone Reached!", April 4, 2025.
2. The JESUS Film Project, "Fact Sheet: JESUS Film Project," Cru, accessed April 4, 2025, https://www.cru.org/us/en/communities /jesus-film-project/fact-sheet.html.
3. Bible Media Group, "The LUMO Project Hits Historical Milestone: Release of 1,000th Language," Bible Media Group, accessed June 4, 2025, https://biblemediagroup.com/lumo-project-milestone/.
4. Faith Comes By Hearing, "Our Impact," Faith Comes By Hearing, accessed April 4, 2025, https://www.faithcomesbyhearing.com/our -impact.
5. BankMyCell, "How Many Phones Are in the World?" January 4, 2025, https://www.bankmycell.com/blog/how-many-phones-are-in -the-world.
6. Global Media Outreach, "Our Impact," Global Media Outreach, accessed April 4, 2025, https://globalmediaoutreach.com/our -impact/.
7. Renew World Outreach, "LightStream: Portable Media Distribution," Renew World Outreach, accessed April 4, 2025, https:// renewoutreach.org/lightstream/.
8. Trans World Radio, "About TWR," TWR, accessed April 4, 2025, https://www.twr.org/about/.
9. SAT-7, "Our Impact," SAT-7, accessed April 4, 2025, https://sat7 usa.org/our-impact/.

Chapter 11

1. Oswald Chambers, "October 17",in *My Utmost for His Highest* (Barbour Publishing, 1988)

Chapter 12

1. Justo L. González, *The Story of Christianity: Volume 1: The Early Church to the Dawn of the Reformation*, rev. ed. (HarperOne, 2010), 173–76.
2. Philip Freeman, *St. Patrick of Ireland: A Biography* (Simon & Schuster, 2005), 120–35.
3. Ruth A. Tucker, *From Jerusalem to Irian Jaya: A Biographical History of Christian Missions*, 2nd ed. (Zondervan, 2004), 58–62.
4. Tucker, *From Jerusalem to Irian Jaya*, 73–76.
5. Tucker, *From Jerusalem to Irian Jaya*, 101–2.
6. David Levering Lewis, *God's Crucible: Islam and the Making of Europe, 570–1215* (W. W. Norton, 2008), 379–81.
7. David Daniell, William Tyndale: A Biography (Yale University Press, 1994), 379–82.
8. C. R. Boxer, *The Christian Century in Japan, 1549–1650* (Berkeley: University of California Press, 1951), 114–19.
9. Justo L. Gonzáles, *The Story of Christianity: Volume 2: The Reformation to the Present Day*, Revised ed. (HarperOne, 2010), 88–92.
10. Courtney Anderson, *To the Golden Shore: The Life of Adoniram Judson* (Judson Press, 1987), 245–68.
11. Tucker, *From Jerusalem to Irian Jaya*, 235–40.
12. Elisabeth Elliot, *Through Gates of Splendor* (Tyndale House, 2005), 174–98.
13. Open Doors, *World Watch List 2009: India Country Report* (Open Doors International, 2009), https://www.opendoors.org.
14. Open Doors, *World Watch List 2024: India Country Report* (Open Doors International, 2024), https://www.opendoors.org.
15. Voice of the Martyrs, "India: Government Restrictions Threaten

Christian Ministries," VOM News, January 15, 2023. https://www
.persecution.com.

16. Open Doors, *World Watch List 2024: Iran Country Report* (Open Doors International, 2024), https://www.opendoors.org.

17. Voice of the Martyrs, "North Korea: Ongoing Persecution of Christians," VOM News, March 10, 2024. https://www.persecution.com.

18. Open Doors, *World Watch List 2024: Somalia Country Report*, (Open Doors International, 2024), https://www.opendoors.org.

19. Open Doors, *World Watch List 2024: Eritrea Country Report*, (Open Doors International, 2024), https://www.opendoors.org.

20. Voice of the Martyrs. "Nigeria: Ongoing Violence Against Christians." VOM News, June 5, 2024. https://www.persecution.com.

21. Open Doors, *World Watch List 2024: Laos Country Report*, (Open Doors International, 2024), https://www.opendoors.org.

22. Open Doors, *World Watch List 2024: China Country Report* (Open Doors International, 2009), https://www.opendoors.org.

23. World Evangelical Alliance. "Religious Liberty Commission Report 2024." Geneva: WEA, 2024. https://worldea.org.

Chapter 13

1. Henley & Partners, *USA Wealth Report 2024*, (Henley & Partners, 2024), https://www.henleyglobal.com/publications/usa-wealth-report -2024.

2. Jim Wise, email message to author, May 8, 2025.

3. MinistryWatch, "Bible Translation Organizations Form Alliance to Translate Bibles." MinistryWatch, March 2021. https://ministry watch.com/bible-translation-organizations-form-alliance-to-translate -bibles/.

4. ACHIEVE Alliance, "Achieve Alliance: It's More Than an Alliance, It's a Movement," accessed May 13, 2025, https://achievealliance.org/.

5. UBS, *Global Wealth Report 2024*, (UBS, 2024), https://www.ubs.com /us/en/wealth-management/insights/global-wealth-report.html.

GREAT COMMISSION MINISTRIES

BIBLE TRANSLATION

American Bible Society	https://americanbible.org
Biblica	https://www.biblica.com
Deaf Bible Society	https://deafbiblesociety.com
Lutheran Bible Translators	https://www.lbt.org
Pioneer Bible Translators	https://pioneerbible.org
Seed Company	https://www.seedcompany.com
SIL International	https://www.sil.org
Spoken Worldwide	https://spoken.org
United Bible Societies	https://www.unitedbiblesocieties.org
unfoldingWord	https://www.unfoldingword.org
The Word for the World	https://twftw.org
Wycliffe Bible Translators	https://www.wycliffe.org

CAMPUS AND STUDENT

Bridges International	https://www.bridgesinternational.com
Chi Alpha	https://chialpha.com

Friends of Internationals	https://www.foi.org
Intervarsity	https://intervarsity.org
Navigators	https://www.navigators.org
Youth With A Mission (YWAM)	https://www.ywam.org

COLLABORATIONS AND NETWORKS

24:14 Coalition	https://2414now.net
ACHIEVE Alliance	https://www.achievealliance.org
Coalition of the Willing	https://coalitionofthewilling.global
Ethne	https://ethne.global
Finishing the Task	https://www.finishingthetask.com
Global Alliance for Church Multiplication	https://www.gacx.io
Illumi*Nations*	https://www.illuminations.bible

CHURCH PLANTING AND DISCIPLE-MAKING

3P Ministries	https://www.3pministries.org
Africa Inland Mission	https://us.aimint.org
All Nations International	https://allnations.international
Biglife	https://big.life
Cru/Global Church Movements	https://www.globalchurchmovements.org
e3 Partners	https://e3partners.org
East-West Ministries	https://www.eastwest.org
Final Command Ministries	https://www.finalcommand.com
Frontiers	https://www.frontiersusa.org
Obedience	https://obedience.life

International Mission Board (IMB)	https://www.imb.org
New Covenant Missions	https://www.newcovenant missions.org
New Generations	https://newgenerations.org
No Place Left	https://noplaceleft.net
Operation Mobilization	https://www.om.org
Pioneers	https://www.pioneers.org
Team Expansion	https://www.teamexpansion.org
The Timothy Initiative	https://www.ttionline.org

DEAF MINISTRY

DOOR International	https://doorinternational.org

IMMIGRANTS AND REFUGEES

Global Frontier Missions	https://globalfrontiermissions.org
Global Gates	https://globalgates.info
Greater Europe Mission	https://www.gemission.org
International Project	https://internationalproject.org
mPower Approach	https://www.mpowerapproach.org
Refugee Oasis	https://www.refugeeoasis.org

FINANCIAL SUPPORT

500K	https://the500k.org
Doulos Partners	https://www.doulospartners.org
The Finishing Fund	https://www.finishingfund.org

MEDIA AND TECHNOLOGY

Audio Scripture Ministries	https://audioscripture.org
Bible Media Group	https://biblemedia.com
Far East Broadcasting Company (FEBC)	https://www.febc.org
Faith Comes by Hearing	https://www.faithcomesbyhearing.com
Elam Ministries	https://www.elam.com
Global Media Outreach	https://www.globalmedia outreach.com
Gospel for Asia	https://www.gfa.org
The JESUS Film	https://www.jesusfilm.org
Mars Hill Productions	https://www.mars-hill.org
MegaVoice	https://www.megavoice.com
Renew World Outreach	https://www.renewoutreach.org
SAT-7	https://www.sat7usa.org
Talking Bibles International	https://www.talkingbibles.org
Trans World Radio (TWR)	https://www.twr.org

PRAYER

110 Cities Prayer Initiative	https://www.110cities.com
24-7 Prayer	https://www.24-7prayer.com
30 Days of Prayer for the Muslim World	https://www.pray30days.org
Global Prayer Resource Network	https://www.globalprn.com
International Prayer Connect (IPC)	https://www.ipcprayer.org
Pray for All	https://prayforall.com

Praying Through the Window   https://www.win1040.org
Prayercast   https://www.prayercast.com

RESEARCH AND AWARENESS

Call2All   https://www.call2all.org
Joshua Project   https://www.joshuaproject.net
Operation World   https://www.operationworld.org
Peoplegroups.org   https://www.peoplegroups.org
The Traveling Team   https://www.thetravelingteam.org

URBAN CHURCH PLANTING

Two Four Eight   https://www.twofoureight.org
Redeemer City to City   https://www.redeemercitytocity.com

ABOUT THE AUTHOR

 Douglas Cobb serves as the managing partner of the Finishing Fund, a partnership of kingdom investors who are giving together to accelerate the completion of the Great Commission. Since 2018 the Fund's partners have invested in ninety projects to send missionaries for the first time to nearly 800 people groups in more than sixty-seven countries.

Doug's first book, *And Then the End Will Come*, considers the promise of Matthew 24:14 and nine other Biblical clues that Jesus is returning soon.

Doug and his wife, Gena, are members of Southeast Christian Church in Louisville, where he teaches the Word by Word Sunday School class and serves as an elder. Gena is a retired Bible Study Fellowship teaching leader.

Doug is a lifelong entrepreneur. In the past he's served as CEO of Appriss, Greater Louisville Inc., and The Cobb Group; as a managing director with Chrysalis Ventures; and as a director for a variety of companies. He is a three-time Inc. 500 CEO and a three-time Kentucky Entrepreneur of the Year.

Doug holds a BA, magna cum laude, from Williams College and an MS in accounting from the New York University Graduate School of Business Administration.

Doug and Gena have been married for forty-five years and have three grown children and six grandchildren.

THE FINISHING FUND

The Finishing Fund is a partnership of generous Christians who are giving together to send missionaries to the last few people groups on earth who do not know Jesus. Our mission is to accelerate the completion of the Great Commission.

Since 2017, 280 donor partners have committed $16.8 million to ninety projects with forty-two ministries to engage nearly 800 people groups in sixty-seven countries with the gospel. The Fund has a minimum investment of $30,000—roughly the cost of a single engagement project. And because the Fund's expenses are covered by its founding partners, 100 percent of each partner's investment goes directly to the field.

For more information, please check out our website at www.finishingfund.org. If you'd like to explore partnership, please email info@finishingfund.org.

STUDY GUIDE

 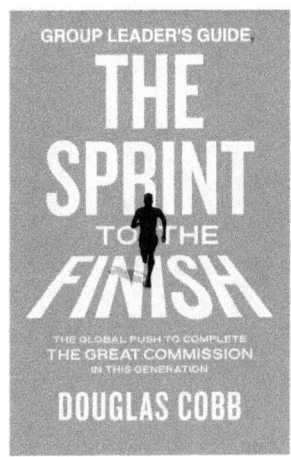

Personal and small group study guides are available for *Sprint to the Finish*.

For more information and other resources, please visit

www.SprintBook.net